A

# VOCABULARY

OF THE

# SÁNTÁLI LANGUAGE

A

# VOCABULARY

OF THE

# SÁNTÁLI LANGUAGE.

BY THE

**REV. E. L. Puxley**

GYAN

*Published by*

Gyan Publishing House
5, Ansari Road
Daryaganj, New Delhi-110002
Phone: 011-47034999, 9811692060
E-mail: books@gyanbooks.com

*Distribution Network*
gyanbooks.com
India, USA, Canada, UK, Australia



ISBN: 978-81-212-7068-7 (HB)
First Published, 1868

2nd Impression 2024

*Printed at:* Gyan Press, Delhi.



**A VOCABULARY OF THE SÁNTÁLI LANGUAGE**
Author: E. L. PUXLEY

A

# VOCABULARY

OF THE

# SÁNTÁLI LANGUAGE.

BY THE

REV. E. L. PUXLEY,

LATE MISSIONARY OF THE CHURCH MISSIONARY SOCIETY
TO THE SANTALS.

PRINTED BY W. M. WATTS,
80, GRAY'S INN ROAD.

1868.

# EXPLANATION.

---

## I.—*Of the letters and diacritical marks used in the Vocabulary.*

In writing Sántáli words I have adopted the system of letters employed by FORBES, SHAKESPEAR, and others, for Roman Hindústáni; and as this system is so well known throughout India, it will be only necessary to explain here those marks and points which are peculiar to the present book, and which I have been compelled to adopt for the representation of sounds peculiar to the Sántáli language.

ạ represents a long, gutteral sound, difficult to describe. It is pronounced very nearly as if it were composed of two short separate *a*'s: for instance, the Sántáli word "bạd" might be written "ba-ad," and, is pronounced somewhat like the English "bird" is by people who speak in an affected way, and drop the sound of the *r*.

occurs only after the final vowel of a word, and takes the place of some consonant which has been dropped; while

" on the other hand, occurs only under the final consonant, which, though not entirely dropped, is very slightly sounded.

These two marks have been sometimes interchanged, *e.g.*, the Sántáli word for "the eye" has been sometimes written "*met*"", and somẹtimes "*me:*"; in the one case, the *t* is slightly heard; in the other, it is inaudible. The former (:) represents a peculiar catch, or jerk, on hearing which, one would suppose that the speaker had suddenly stopped to correct himself.

## II.—*Of the signs used after the Sántáli words in the Vocabulary.*

† after some words, denotes that the word so marked belongs to some other Indian language.

° denotes that the word is derived from some other Indian language.

? after either a Sántáli or an English word, denotes that I have some doubt as to its correctness.

* occuring after the names of trees, plants, insects, &c., denotes that it is one of a list of such words which I made some years ago; but, as I overlooked this list when revising the manuscript of the Vocabulary, I do not feel certain that the words of it are correctly spelt or correctly translated.*

## III.—*Of the forms of Verbs as given in the Vocabulary.*

When possible, the verb has been made to agree with a nominative case of the common gender and third person singular, and the future and past tenses of the neuter and transitive forms have been given. Transitive verbs also are made (when possible) to govern an accusative case of the third person singular and of the common gender, as "*ábo:ái, áp,, enái, kedeái,*" †

Sometimes, however, I have been compelled to depart from this arrangement, for—

* The mention of such words, notwithstanding the doubt attached to them, may be of some service to those who come after me in this field; and therefore I have thought it advisable to insert them.

† In Sántáli a transitive verb agrees, in number, gender, and person, with the word it governs, as well as with the word with which it agrees (or with what we may call its accusative, as well as with its nominative); to effect this agreement two changes occur in the verb, one in the middle, and one at the termination.

Some verbs require that the nominative case with which they agree, and the accusative case which they govern, should either, or both, be in the plural or dual number; and sometimes, again, verbs conjugated as active do not govern an accusative case at all: as "*áchhím kedái*," "he sneezed."

Other verbs can only be conjugated as active, *e.g.*, "*achui eái, achu kedeái.*"

Others, again, are only neuter, as "*aple:ái, aple enái.*"

Sometimes, when such would be its ordinary use, the verb has been put into the dative form, in one or other of the tenses, as "*áchbícho:ái, áchbích enái, ádeái; ájári ái ái, ádeái.*"

Jingling verbs, such as *phás phús, uk buk,* are of very frequent occurrence: for the sake of brevity, I have only repeated the second of these words in the past tenses, as "*akbakáu:ái; bakáu enái.*"

Double verbs (*i.e.*, two verbs formed into, or used as, one) are also common: here I have simply mentioned the root, as the past tenses of such words may be easily discovered, by referring to the latter of the two verbs in its own place.

Occasionally the simple root of a verb, without any tenses, may be met with; the explanation of this is, that not having ever heard of the past tenses of such words, I preferred not to mention anything of which I did not feel tolerably certain.

It should also be remarked, that many transitive verbs, which have been put down in the Vocabulary as forming their perfect tenses in "*ked*" would also require, in speaking, the causal verb *ocho;* as a very slight acquaintance with the language would enable a speaker to put the causal verb in its right place; and, as this is a point more for a Grammar than a Dictionary, I have not thought it necessary to insert it, except when it was absolutely required.

As most verbs may, in Sántáli, be conjugated either as neuter or transitive, I have, in rendering them into English, mixed together the neuter and transitive signification of them; *e.g.*, "*achuro:*," "walk about, move about, repent, restore, bring back."

---

## POSTSCRIPT.

The letters '*n̲r*' are throughout the Vocabulary the representatives of *one* Bengáli letter; the *n* is nasal, and the *r* to be pronounced as if written *ṛ*.

## A

*Á:*, bow

*Á: sár*, bow and arrow

*A:a*, ? break down

*Ạạn*, ° law

*Abdán*, ? master

*Abhágiya*, † luckless, unfortunate

*Abhrá:*, lake, water, piece of water

*Ábo:ái, áp" enái, kedeái*, alight, wash the face

*Abolá*, ° beast, dumb animal

*Aboṛ bodhai eái, kedeái*, flatter, wheedle

*Ábuko:ái, ábuk enái, kedeái*, wash the hands

*Achár bichár*, conduct, life, walk and conversation

*Áchbícho:ái, áchbích enái, ádeái*, despise, scorn, loathe, hate, turn from in disgust

*Áchel páchel*, wealth, splendour, grandeur

*Áchhímo:ái, áchhím enái, kedái*, sneeze

*Achká:ái, achká enái, kedeái*, surprise, startle, not to expect

*Achkáte, achkági*, suddenly, unexpectedly, accidentally

*Achkámạr*, sudden

*Achráu*, to sow a field with rice to be afterwards transplanted

*Achui eai, achu kedeái*, engage labourers, employ, give employment

*Achuro:ái, achur enái, kedeái*, walk about or round, move about, repeat, bring back, restore, answer

*Achur ruaṛ*, reward, repay, revenge

*Ạd*, the beginning

*Ạd chalí*, original custom, old tradition

*Ạd khoná:*, from eternity

*Ádo:ái, át„ enái, kedeai*, lose, forfeit, mistake, lose the way

*Ádá*, a measure (about seven bushels)

*Áḍá*, a shelter for cattle from the mid-day sun, a shed

*Ádá: á, ádái ená, ádá kedái*, to be seasoned (with salt, &c.), rub in (oil, &c.)

*Ádá báṛi*, tend silkworms

*Ádáingn ái, ádáing kedái*, gain, make a profit

*Ádár*, lust, heat (of animals)

*Áḍepáse*, neighbouring, near

*Áḍepáserenko*, neighbours

*Áder eái, kedeái*, shew hospitality, take in, admit

*Aḍger*, to go

*Ádh*, ? dear, costly

*Ádhá gnindá*, midnight

*Ádhán*, some, a little, half

*Ádhár*, fodder, provision

*Ádh baisure*,° at half age, prematurely

*Ádhi:á, ádhi ená, kedeái*, lessen, diminish, abate

*Adherom*,° irreligious, wicked

*Adhua*, without the Sántál marks on the left arm

*Aḍi*, much, many, very

*Aḍi gárte*, noisily, fast, violently, loudly, strongly

*Aḍi utaṛ*, very many, abundant

*Aḍi baṛi:*, very much

*Aḍi okoi:*, a good deal

*Aḍi chhoṭ* } often
*Aḍi dháu* }

*Aḍi aḍi* } many kinds
*Aḍi tirit* }

*Ádo*, and, moreover

*Aḍo jong*, make water, pass [urine

*Ádom*, some, a little, a few

*Ádop*„ influence, effect, intention

*Aduá*, rice eaten without boiling

*Áedári*, inheritance, possession, authority

*Afsor*,° means, opportunity

*Afsoro:*, obtain opportunity

*Agilo: á, agil ená, kedái*, load a cart too heavy in front

*Agnui*, to give to drink, gild, cover (with gold, &c.)

*Agui eái, agu kedeái*, bring, fetch, take (life)

*Agu daṛái*, bring, come bringing

*Agu oṭo*, restore

*Agu ocho*, send for

*Ahá*, alas!

*Ahá:ái, ahái enái, ahá kedái*, be bewitched. [It is thought that when one who has eaten filth in his childhood looks on another eating, he vomits]

*Ahakáu:ái, ahakáu enái, kedái,* pant

*Áhár,* a dam, bank

*Áhaṛí,* tender of silkworms

*Ahináu:á, ahináu enái, kedái,* commence to rot, begin to corrupt or spoil

*Aho,* no, not

*Ahongkár,*° pride

*Ái:, ái: gi,* own, himself

*Ái:á, ái ená, kedái,* guess, measure, ascertain

*Áiháu:ái, áikáu ená, kedeái,* grope in the dark, guess, perceive, taste, experience, feel, seem, appear

*Áikáu thík,* discover, settle

*Áiháu gelá,* test, try

*Ạil mạilte,* disorderly

*Ạil mạilo: á, ạil mạil ená, kedeái,* confuse, put into confusion, disorder

*Áimá,* much, many

*Áimái,* woman

*Ainomo: á, ainom enái, kedeái,* paint round the eyes, apply 'ainom' to the eyes

*Áiomán,* ? select, appropriate

*Ájár,* ? ill, sick, diseased

*Ájári ái ái, ádeái,* call on, visit, have an interview with

*Ajátiya,*° outcast

*Ajauṛi,* empty

*Ájbíjá:, ájbíá:,* right, proper, due

*Ajhánṭo:ái, ajhánṭ enái, kedeái,* use force, be violent

*Ajo áiái, ádeái,* feed (another), nurse

*Akái ái, aká kedeái,* suspend, hang up

*Akál,* † famine, scarcity

*Akáuná,* a shrub ?

*Akbakáu:ái, bakáu enái, kedeái,* discomfit, set in confusion, be in trouble, pant, suffer from heat

*Akhạini,* pitchfork, forked stick

*Akhírre,*° finally, lastly, afterwards

*Ákíl,*° wise, learned

*Ákíl bud,*° wisdom, knowledge

*Akkáji,* to swear; take an oath

*Ákote,* by their own accord

*Ákringno:á, ákringn ená, ákring kedái,* sell, dispose of

*Ákudo: á, ákut„ enái, kedeái,* be quick, hasten, be in a fuss

*Ákut„ bákut„,* difficult (used of a stony, thorny, hilly road)

*Alái áiái, enái, alá kedeái,* surrender, give over or up, put for a prize

*Áláng,* the tongue

*Alát,, olodo:ái, olot,, enái, kedeái*, be confused in talking, contradict one's self

*Aláundhá*, dazzled, scarcely seeing (as one coming into a strong light)

*Álbudahá*, *Áldhundhahá*, { senseless, animal-like, beastly

*Álgá*, easy, convenient

*Álgáte*, easily

*Alo*, not (with imperative and subjunctive moods)

*Amáli eái, enái, kedeái*,° give authority to

*Ambá: ambogo:ái, ambo: enái, kedeái*, roll from side to side, waddle like a drunkard

*Ámdá*, a division of the country [the part of the country which a man knows well is his 'ámdá']

*Amdáj ái, kedái*, ° guess

*Ámlá*, † court officers

*Ámlá kaplá*, ditto

*Ám míká dar*, five-leaved mango branch, with which the jog manjhi sprinkles the young couple at weddings

*Aṇ*,° law (see also *ạạn*)

*Anạri*,° stranger

*Anbhul*, unconscious, out of senses

*Anchár*,° hem, edge of dress, fringe, border of dress

*Ancháu*, ? to offer sacrifice, present in sacrifice

*Andá: tawágo:ái, tawá: enái, kedeái*, go astray, be missing, not to find, discomfit, confound

*Anḍár onḍoro:ái, ondor enái, kedeái*, be confused, lose the way, be caught in a storm, be astonished, stare, open the eyes in astonishment

*Andhá eái, andhái enái, andhá kedeai*, deal deceitfully, delude

*Andhá dhund eái, kedeái*, oppress, make great disturbance

*Anḍiá*, bull, male

*Anḍijo:ái, anḍi: enai, kedeái*, deceive, coax, wheedle, seduce, inveigle, defraud

*Ándmándáu:ái, mándáu enái, kedeái*, be troubled, perplexed

*Andoro: á, andor ená, kedái*, sound, report, make a row, make noise

*Andrá*, half blind, having dull [eyes

*Andu: mandu:* frightened, startled, looking all round

*Ané: dhánejo:ai, dháne: enai, kedeai*, have plenty, be wealthy, affluent, have abundance

*Angáu:ái, angáu enai, kedái*, admit, confess

*Angeno:*, to disappear for ever in a haunted tank

*Angíro:ái, angír enái, kedeái*, elope with (a girl), carry off (a woman)

*Angoicho:ái, angoich enái, kedái*, admit, confess

*Angop,, angobo:ái, angop,, enái, kedái*, gasp as a dying person, sigh, yawn

*Angrop*, a jacket, "kurta"

*Ani:* with (in compos) as *búdáni:* wise, *úpáni:* hairy

*Anjedo:á, anjet,, enái, kedái*, dry up (as a river)

*Anjle:ái, anjle enái, kedái*, hold the hands open to catch something

*Anjomo: á, anjom enái, kedeái, áděái*, hear, listen, grant, obey, address, accede

*Anjom orom*, know or understand from hearing

*Án̲rgátre*, early, before the usual time (supposing that something is to be done afterwards)

*Án̲rgo:ái* / *Án̲rgun ái* } *Án̲rgoi enái, án̲rgo kedeái*, descend, take down

*Án̲rgom*, harrow (a flat and long piece of wood used in breaking the clods of newly-ploughed fields)

*Án̲rkus kathá*, stirring up, reproach, words of chiding

*Án̲rti áiái, ádeái*, help a second time to food

*Ansái ái, ansá kedái*, make a noise

*Ánṭ*, hard, difficult, requiring force, loud

*Ánṭhoe*, a storm, strong wind

*Ánṭo:ái, ánṭ enái, kedái*, do something quickly, or strongly

*Anṭáu: á, anṭáu ená, kedeái*, suffice, be contained, divide? hold out

*Aṇwṭhá*, a ring for the great toe

*Apábaria: áko, bará enáko, ket koái*, separate, divide, part asunder

*Apájo: ákin, apáj enákin*, concede precedence, respect

*Ápán ápín*,° mutual, several, respective

*Ápán ápíno: ákin, ápín enákin, ket koái,* assume different sides, mutually separate

*Apạri,* arrow-head

*Áphím,*†, opium

*Aphṭau: ákin, aphṭáu enákin, ket koái,* challenge, provoke

*Ápiro:á, ápir ená, kedái,* fly off obliquely

*Aple:ai, aple enái,* climb a smooth tree by legs and arms

*Apná apní,* mutual, several, respective

*Áp,,napáio:* wash clean(the face)

*Apnár,*° own (my own, thy own, &c., according to the nom. of the verb)

*Ápuing, ápum, ápát,,,* my, thy, his father

*Ár,* and, also, again, other

*Árhoṇ,* again, also, more, other, moreover

*Árá,* red

*Árá upál,* the red lily

*Ạrá:,* greens, potatoes [tables

*Ạrá:sákám,* greens, vege-

*Ạrágái, áṛá: enái, kedeái,* free, set at liberty, escape, leave, loosen, abate, discharge, let-off gun, &c.

*Ạṛáng,* voice, sound

*Aṛáni,* * a measure so called

*Áráṇr,* a yoke

*Árdá,* unploughed(ground)fresh

*Áṛe,* edge

*Áṛerenko,* neighbours

*Árẹjo: á, áre: ená, kedái,* water (by baling up the water in hands or in a "*chiṭai*")

*Árel,* hailstone

*Aṛi:,* ? rice-field in ridges

*Ari ái, kedái,* ordain, appoint

*Áríd ai,árit,,kedái,* look aslant, watch another stealthily

*Arik parik,* very cleanly

*Áṛing ái, áṛiṇ kedái,* strain off water from cooked rice

*Áríso:ái, árís enái, kedeái,* scream,? make a noise,? be vexed, bothered, tired, give offence

*Arján,* populous, cultivated

*Arján eái, enái, kedeái,* goad, spur, spear

*Arjáu: á, arjáu ená, kedái,* gain, make profit

*Aṛjháu: á, aṛjháu ená, kedeái,* be entangled, run against, entrap [plain

*Arji ái, kedái,*° request, com-

*Arojo:ái, aroj kedái,*° make an application, beg, beseech

*Árpá,* a fathom, the stretch of the arms, the bundle of rice paid for cutting it

*Arṛáu:ái, arṛáu enái, kedái*, bellow (as a buffalo), roar

*Arsí*, glass, mirror

*Árubo:ái, árup„ ená, kedeái*, wash (rice, &c.), wash away, (as by a flood)

*Árup„ safhá* } wash clean
*Árup„ poṇḍ* }

*Ás*,† hope, desire, trust

*Áso:ái, ás enái, kedeái*, hope, trust, encourage, take refuge

*Ás chhuṭáu:*, be disappointed, despair

*Asambher*, illimitable

*Ásámí*, defendent, borrower, client

*Ásen eái, kedeái*, tend (a child, &c.), carry about, lead about

*Áse: táse:*, plentiful, very rich, luxuriant

*Asírbád*,† blessing

*Asírbád em*, bless

*Áshandaní*, crying greatly, peevish (a child)

*Ásket*,° lazy

*Ásol*,° chief, principal

*Áso khái: te*, especially

*Ásrá:ái, ásrái enái, ásrá kedeái*,† hope, trust, animate, encourage

*Assis*,† curse

*Asukh*,† discomfort, disquiet

*Asúlo:ái, asúl enái, kedeái*, support, nourish, take care of, nurse

*Asúl hopon*, adopted son

*Ásúr*, glutton

*Aswári*,° cavalry, rider

*Atái ai, ená, atá kedeái*, fry, parch, bake

*Áṭál*, layer, row

*Áṭál sákám*, leaves of a book

*Bár áṭál*, twofold, doubled

*Áṭál bahá*,* kind of flower

*Átángo :á, átáng kedái*, take, catch (in hands or vessel), take something into open hand, put hand under (something to support it)

*Átáro: á, átár enái, kedeái*, set on fire, burn jungle

*Áṭedo: á, áṭet„ ená, kedái*, spread out (*e.g.* sheet, &c.)

*Áṭet„ á:*, bed-clothes

*Aten ái, kedái*, listen, hear secretly, bend the ear (to listen)

*Athán dá:*, a flood (from overflowing of rivers), very deep water

*Athel*,* a kind of tree 'athela'

*Aṭhreno: á, áṭhren enái, kedeái*, prop up the body, support from beneath

*Áting*, to feed (as cattle), graze

*Aṭkáro:ái, aṭhár enái, kedeái*, prove, try, test, feel

*Aṭkáu: á, aṭkáu enái, kedeái*,[o] obstruct, hinder, prevent

*Áṭhir eái, kedeái*, carry off

*Áṭkuṛá*, sonless, heirless

*Áṭkuṭí*, thistles

*Átmá*,† spirit, soul

*Átná*, a kind of tree

*Áto*, village, hamlet

*Átrá: á, átrái enái, átrá kedeái*, miss, fail to obtain, fail to reach

*Atruingno:ái, atruingn enái atruing kedeái*, be dissatisfied, dislike

*Átu*, flood

*Átu:ái, átui ená, átu kedái*, float, flow, run (as water)

*Átu: gaḍá*, bed of river

*Aturo:ái, atur enái, kedeái*, trail along

*Aṭwár din*,[o] Sunday

*Audá*, meditation, intention

*Audá jong*, be prudent, farseeing

*Auṇsá bauṇsá*, race, lineage, descendants

*Auri*, soon, before, not yet

*Auṛiá*, uselessly, falsely, causelessly, idly, in vain

*Ausáno:ái, ausán enái, kedeái*, obtain ease, rest, lighten, alleviate, mitigate, recover, assist

*Aután*, fort,? concealed spot, safe retreat, strong place suitable for fighting in

*Awátappá:ái, tappái enái, tappá kedeái*, be in distress

*Áyám bing*, a snake, the cobra

*Ayogi*, hallo! indeed! O my! dear me!

*Áyup*, evening

*Áyup payár*, evening

## B

*Bá*, no, not, (in compos, as *báing, bám, bái*, &c.)

*Báng*, no, not

*Báb ái, ádeái*, order, petition, request, speak

*Bábádo:, bábát„ enái*, have the itch

*Bábái á:*, case (in which to keep things)

*Bábár*, by two's, two and two

*Báber*, rope

*Bábu*, term used in addressing an inferior or younger person

*Bábur*,† a thorney tree like mimosá

*Bachhá*,[o] bull calf

*Bachhi*, heifer

*Bachháu:ái, bachháu enái, kedeai*, pick out, select, choose

*Bachháu tod..*, select (out of many)

*Bachkạr*, harlot, prostitute, courtezan (a caste)

*Báchkom*, grass rope, coarse grass, used for beds, chairs, &c.

*Bachláu:ái, bachláu enái, kedeái*, preserve, defend, be safe, save, escape

*Bád, bádí*, accuser, enemy, opponent, hatred

*Bạd ái, kedeái*, cultivate

*Bạd*, a plain-like field

*Baḍạí*, boastful, arrogant; pride, vainglory, conceit

*Badáṇw, badisti*, enmity, ill-feeling, ill-wishing

*Baḍáio: á, baḍái enái, kedeái*, appear, be known

*Báde háláng*, draw out warp in weaving

*Badhá*, wooden sandals

*Khunṭi badhá*, high ditto

*Bạḍháu: á, bạḍháu enái, kedeái*,° promote, increase

*Badhí: á, badhí enái, kedeái*, bind up, wind up, wrap up

*Badhistí*, rival

*Baḍhohí*,° carpenter, mason

*Badot*, evil

*Bagáhí*,° tiger which has killed many people

*Bagdáu: á, bagdáu enái, kedeái*, miss, fail, forget something, lose the way

*Bághin*,* thorn bush

*Bagí: á, bagí enái, kedeái*, quit, abandon, forsake, leave

*Bágwán*, garden of mangoes

*Bahá*, flower

*Bahá: a, bahái enái, kedeái*, flower, bloom, adorn with flowers

*Bahá din*, festival

*Bahá kochá*, flowẹr-garden

*Bahá gutui*, to weave a garland

*Bahá saṇwhá*, to marry a second time

*Bahálo:ái, bahál enái, kedeái*,° be appointed, restored to one's position

*Báhaná: gnutum*, surname, nickname, the name by which an individual is usually known, though not his original one

*Baháu:ái, baháu enái, kedeái*, live, exist, last, support

*Bahire*,° external, outer

*Bahire se:*, outside

*Bahní*,° whirlpool

*Bahú,* wife, bride, daughter-in-law

*Bahú áiái, kedeái* / *Bahú agui* — to marry a wife

*Bạị,?* age

*Bái ái, kedeái,* take care of, keep, preserve safely

*Bai baite,* softly, gently

*Bainá,*° advances of money

*Bạio: ái, bại enái,*† be delirious, be sick of "bai"

*Bairi,*† enemy

*Baisáu: á, baisáu enái, kedeái,* lend on usury, fix, appoint, settle, let out, hire out, establish, be firm

*Bájár,*° bazaar, market, city, town

*Bajáu:ái, bajáu enái, kedeái,* hit against, receive a blow, knock or strike against (*e. g.* wind), come in contact with, affect (*e. g.* sickness)

*Bají:ái, bají enái, kedeái,* turn a summersault

*Báju,* armlet, brass or tin ornaments or charms, worn on the arm

*Bák,*† crane

*Bákát, bukudo:ái, bukut" enái, kedeái,* quicken (as fœtus in the womb)

*Bakáu:ái, bakáu enái, kedeái,* inspire, put into the mind, speak thoughtlessly, let something slip out of the mouth

*Bakhanáu:ái, bakhanáu enái, kedeái,* give obscene abuse

*Bákhe̲n̲r ái, ádeái,* pray (to Satan) invoke

*Bakher* / *Bakhol* — a double house with enclosure between, house and garden, court, establishment

*Bakhoro:ái, bakhor kedái,* transplant

*Báki,*† remainder

*Bák junú,* firefly

*Báklá:,* bark, peel, rind

*Baksís,*° gift, present, favour

*Bákyá,* trumpet

*Bálá erá,** son's wife's mother, daughter's husband's mother

*Bálbaláu:ái, bálbaláu enái,* sweat, perspire

*Bále,* young, tender, delicate

*Bále gidirá,* young child, baby

*Bále dábi,* gristle at the end of collar-bone, cartilege

*Bále molo,* new moon

*Balidán,*† offerings, sacrifice

*Bálo: á, bál enái, kedeái*, open (a boil, &c.), make a hole with red-hot iron

*Bámber*, torch

*Bambkáu: á, bambkáu ená*, kindle, blaze up

*Báná*, a bear; a kind of bird

*Báná:*, bush-hook

*Bánám*, kind of banjo made of wood, with one string

*Bánám ái, kedái*, play the "bánám"

*Bánár*, both

*Bánár se:*, in both directions, on either hand

*Bánátok*,* a kind of tree

*Bánbasi*, deluge, flood

*Bancháu:ái, bancháu enái*,[o] *kedeái*, live, survive, preserve, defend, save

*Bánd*,[o] bank, embankment

*Bánd tol*, to raise a bank

*Bándá*, birdlime, the tree from which birdlime is extracted

*Bánde:ái, bánde enái, kedeái*, put on clothes (woman), dress (woman)

*Bándhok*,† pledge, token

*Bándhono:ái, bándhon enái, kedeái*, fascinate, charm, bind with securities, take security

*Bándí*, large straw-rope baskets in which "dhán" is kept

*Bandịá*, bull with short tail

*Bándo narí*, wild vine, a creeper

*Bandpará*,* a snake that crawls either way

*Bandúk*,† gun

*Báng*, no, not

*Bángmá*, viz., that is, i.e.

*Bángkhán*, unless, otherwise, or else, even

*Báng ákil*, stupid

*Báng jo*, barren, fruitless

*Báng bororá*, not clean (as half-washed clothes)

*Báng muchạt*,,, endless, eternal

*Báng goju: i:*, immortal

*Báng dosi:*, innocent

*Báng patiáu*, to disbelieve

*Báng gáno:*, be impossible

*Báng táhen*, be absent

*Báng dayái:* cruel, unmerciful, inexorable, unrelenting

*Báng khusí* / *saná* } dislike, be dissatisfied

*Báng jurí:* / *mído:* / *tulujo:* / *gnápámo:* } disagree

*Báng disạ̣i*, be delirious, be out of one's senses

*Báng gog*,,, deny

*Báng reben*, decline

*Báng hilo:*,? uncultivated

*Bang lángá:*, be indefatigable

*Báng lájáu:*, be shameless

*Báng bichạr*, be thoughtless

*Báng dáṛe*, be unable

*Báng hopon áni: hopono: i:* } barren (animals), childless

*Bangáurá*, cotton-seed

*Bạṇh áiái, ádeái*, stir-up, excite

*Bánjhí*,° barren (woman)

*Bánká*, bent, curved

*Bankí*, anklet

*Bánriá*,* "kohndá" a kind of pumpkin

*Bánrsi*,† fishhook

*Bánu:*, is not, not to exist, (only in present tense)

*Banwáṭo: á, banwáṭ ená, kedái*, to return to jungle again

*Banyá*†, trader

*Báonre*, reel of cotton, two sticks like a V

*Bápágo: ákin, bápá: enákin, ketkinái*, separate, part (as man and wife), break-off friendship

*Báphau: á, báphau ena, kedái*,° boil, steam

*Báplá*, marriage, wedding

*Báplá: ákin, báplá enákin*, marry

*Bápuṛi:*, poor, wretched, miserable

*Bár*, two

*Bár jíwí ákán*, pregnant

*Bár mochá*, two-faced, hypocritical

*Bár mon*, deceitful, changeable, fickle

*Bár pạilá*, a measure about a quart

*Barábar*,† even, equal, uniform, level

*Barábariren*, mediator, umpire, one who stands between

*Báráhí*, thick rope

*Baṛáio: á, baṛái kedái*, appear, be known, know, understand, suppose, think (see also *baḍáio:*)

*Bárdunruṇi:*, bat, flying fox

*Báṛe*, banyan tree

*Báreto:ái, báret enái*,' *kedeái*, accompany the bride to her husband's village or house

*Báṛgi*, field, garden

*Baṛháu,*[o] increase (see *baḍháu*)

*Baṛi:*, bad, evil, wicked, sinful, injury, defect

*Baṛi: kamí*, misconduct, fault

*Baṛi: kamí hoṛ* / *Baṛi: i:* { misconducted, an evil person

*Baṛijo:ái, baṛi: enái, kedeái*, injure, be guilty, corrupt, destroy

*Baṛi: men*, to abuse, slander

*Bariạt,*[o] wedding guests, wife's brothers

*Bárkáite*, dissembling, mockingly

*Bárki*, sheet, "dohar"

*Báro hoṛo*, early rice

*Bár phúl,** a white flower

*Bárte ái, kedái*, notify a hunt, publish

*Baṛtí*, more

*Bárti ái, ádeái*, give generously (with both hands)

*Baru,** oil tree

*Baruḍáng*, toad, large frog

*Bạs*, age

*Básángo: á, básáng enái, kedái*, heat (water), warm (water)

*Báske daká,*[o] rice kept from the preceding day

*Báskiá jom*, break fast

*Báskiá ber* / *Básiám ber* } about nine o'clock

*Báso: á, bás enái, kedeái*, emit odour, smell badly, stink

*Básudo:ai, básut,, enái, ádeái*, regard highly, reverence, respect, think well of

*Baṭá: baṭágo:ái, baṭá: enái, kedeái*, writhe (as a dying person)

*Batáu ái, kedái*, acknowledge, confess, obey, regard

*Baṭi*, cup

*Bát katáu,*[o] disprove, disobey, stop (another) in speaking

*Batláu áiái, ádeái,*[o] teach, show

*Baṭrí*, toe ornament (three rings which produce a jingling)

*Battí,*† lamp

*Báuláu:ái, báuláu enái*, rave, become insane, be very drunk, very angry

*Bauṉrá,*† stumpy, sturdy, a a dwarf

*Báuṉsá,*[o] race, lineage, descendents

*Báyábán*, inundation, flood

*Báyár*, male buffalo, bull

*Beáj,*† interest on money

*Bebenáui:, be: náui:*, creator, maker

*Bebhorsá,*° disappointed

*Beḍá,* field, low land near river

*Beḍaul,*† shapeless

*Bedhá,* crabbed, knotty

*Beḍhái, beṛhái,* all round, on all sides

*Bedháu:ái, bedháu enái, kedeái,* wind round, wrap round

*Bedisá,* careless, thoughtless

*Bedo:ái, bet,, enái, kedeái,* hoodwink, blindfold, cover the face or mouth

*Befáida,*† in vain, useless, fruitless

*Begár,*° separately, apart, asunder

*Begáro: á, begár enái, kedeái,* separate, set apart

*Begár idí,* carry off by force

*Begár begár,* distinguish between

*Begor,*° except, unless, without

*Behál,*° astonishing, extraordinary

*Behudís,* thoughtless

*Beíá,* causeless, useless

*Bejhá,* target

*Bejhái ái, bejhá kedái,* aim at

*Bejo:ái, be:kedái,* vomit

*Bekám,*° useless, causeless, idle

*Belá,*° time

*Belá machhá,* proper season

*Bele,* egg

*Bele ái, kedái,* lay eggs

*Bele:,* ripe

*Bele: á, bele ená, hedái,* ripen

*Belkeng,*? leaf, letter [set up

*Belo: á, bel ená, kedái,* establish,

*Belogo: á, belog,, ená, kedeái,* give way

*Belteng,* very small

*Belteng galái,* a collection of small insects

*Bená,** kind of grass

*Benáhak,*° useless, causeless

*Benáu ái, kedeái,*° make, create, form

*Beṇḍáu: á, beṇḍáu enái, kedeái,* kill, destroy, perish

*Beneá,* adversary, enemy

*Benged ái, benget,, kedeái,* gaze, stare, spy, watch, be kind to, pity, help

*Benget,, ruaṛo:,* look back

*Benget,, phariạ,* have one's eyesight restored

*Bepenged,* stare mutually, mutually spy, squint at each other

*Beṉrbágo:ái, beṉrbá: enái, kedeái,* stammer, lisp, stutter

*Beṇt,*† cane, ratan

*Bentáro:ái, bentár enai, kedeái,* tie on (clothes, &c.)

*Ber, berá,*[o] season, time

*Ber hásuro:,* set (as sun)

*Ber rákáb,* rise (as sun)

*Ber he ber,* seasonably

*Berá berí,* staring round (in anger), angrily stamping about

*Beredái, beret,, enái, kedeái,* lift up, raise, awake, be or make well

*Beret,, ruaṛo,* rise again, recover

*Berel,* raw, uncooked, cold (water)

*Berelo: á, berel enái, kedeái,* live, dwell

*Bergá,* dwarf (used in anger)

*Beṛhái se:,* all round, on all sides. See also *beḍhái*

*Berhon,* daily wages

*Berthá,*[o] impossible, in vain

*Bes,*† right, good, better, proper

*Beso: á, bes enái, kedeái,* to be or make good

*Bes okoi:te,* well, properly

*Besáu eái, kedeái,* mock, mimic

*Beshorom, besrom,*[o] shameless, bold, forward

*Besímạ,*[o] boundless

*Besoṇk,* breathless

*Besorá,** a bird so called (of prey)

*Bethá,* disease of the liver, soreness of the whole body, especially on loins

*Beṭhikána,*† careless, thoughtless, uncertain, in the dark

*Bhábná,* affliction, sorrow

*Bhábná:ái, bhábná enái, kedeái,* be afflicted, be concerned, feel anxious, be dejected

*Bhachkáu:ái, bhachkáu enái kedeái,* rave, chatter

*Bhádeso:ái, bhádes enái kedeái,* use irony, ridicule, sneer, despise, revile, slander, abuse, deceive, make pretences

*Bhádo:ái, bhát,, enái, kedeái,* be satisfied, have a belly full

*Bhádu,** a kind of tree so called

*Bhagáu:ái, bhagáu enái, kedeái,*[o] overcome, put to flight

*Bhági,* good, well, excellent, proper

*Bhági sabit,,te*
*Bhági lekáte*
*Bhági sahiṇtte* } properly, well

*Bhagnái,* sister's son

*Bhagwá:ái, bhagwái enái, bhagwá kedeái,* wear the "nangoti"

*Bháincháing* (*m-t*) my (thy, his) elder brother's son

*Bhaján*, pot, pitcher, vessel

*Bhákhá*,† language, spoken dialect

*Bhalá*,† just! well then!

*Bhálogo:ái*, *bhálo: enái*, *kedeái*, be mad, insane, rabid

*Bhálo: setá*, mad dog

*Bhalwá*, a swallow (bird)

*Bhándán*, ceremonies of purification after death of a friend

*Bhanḍár*,† granary, storehouse

*Bhanduṛo:ái*, *bhanduṛ enái*, *kedeái*, to undress (as a woman whose *sáṛhi* has fallen)

*Bhanḍur ái*, *kedái*, waste time, remain idle

*Bháng*,† hemp for smoking

*Bhángáṭo: á*, *bhángáṭ ená*, *kedái*, be ruined, abandoned (as a field with broken banks)

*Bhangalá bháṭo:* be destroyed, be desolate

*Bhangwá*, idle

*Bhanjáu:ái*, *bhanjáu enái*, *kedeái*,° exercise the body, change money

*Bhankṭáu:á*, *bhankṭáu enái*, *kedeái*, set astray, deceive

*Bháo*,† rate, price

*Bhaoṛtiá*,* an antelope of that name

*Bhárá*,† fare, rent, tax

*Bhárábháṭo:á*, *bháṭ enái*, *kedeái*, die, sustain loss, perish, spend in vain

*Bharanḍo*, whirlwind

*Bharáṉring*, bee

*Bharí*, employment, work for labourers, wages, food

*Bharí*,° difficult, heavy

*Bharí hoṛmo*, pregnant

*Bharí: á*, *bharí enái*, *kedeái*, load (a cart, &c.)

*Bháriạ ái*, *kedái*, carry on the shoulder

*Bháro:ai*, *bhároi enái*, *bháro kedeái*, be astonished, be amazed, wonder

*Bhartí: á*, *bhartí enái*, *kedeái*,† be pregnant, be admitted, be filled

*Bharuṉro:ái*, *bharuṉr enái*, *kedeái*, unravel, become loose, become thin (*e.g.* rope)

*Bhasí:ái*, *bhasí enái*, *kedeái*, form habits, become accustomed to

*Bhatáu:á*, *bhatáu ená*, *kedái*, fill up, level

*Bháti*,? bellows

*Bhauṉrá:á*, *bhauṉrái ená*, *bhauṉrá kedái*, bore a hole (with gimlet, &c.)

*Bhayádi*,° family, relations

*Bhed,*† gist, secret, meaning, essence

*Bheḍá, bheḍí,** ram, ewe

*Bhejá,*† subscription, collection

*Bhejá kouḍi,* ditto

*Bhekbheko:ái, bhek enái, kedeái,* chatter, talk much, repeat over and over

*Bhembhá,* foolish, ignorant

*Bhen,* to mourn, weep, wail for the dead

*Bheoná,* a vision

*Bhibiko:ái, bhibik enái, kedeái,* be indignant

*Bhíjáu: á, bhíjáu ená, kedeái,* operate (medicine), influence, have effect upon, overcome (sorrow, &c.)

*Bhiná: á, bhiná enái, kedeái,* separate, distinguish

*Bhingṛáu: áko, bhingṛáu enáko, kethoái,* break-up (an assembly), abandon (purpose)

*Bhiṛáu,* to cleave, stick

*Bhiri jáe,** a kind of grass

*Bhiriko:ái, bhirik enái kedeái,* start back, be disgusted, dislike

*Bhiṛkáu:ái, bhirháu enái, kedeái,* frighten, startle, surprise, terrify (see also *biṛkáu*)

*Bhít,*† wall

*Bhítrí,*° inside, inner

*Bhítríte,* within

*Bhochbhocháu:ái, bhocháu enái, kedeái,* chatter, scold, talk incoherently

*Bhodor,* unrepaired, abandoned; to fail, abandon

*Bhog ái, bho: kedái,* bark (as a dog)

*Bhogáu:ái, bhogáu enái, kedeái,* be corpulent

*Bhogoj, bhoj,*† feast

*Bhoj ái, kedái,* feast

*Bhokhár,*† sheath of sword

*Bhokráu ái, kedái,* low (as a cow, &c.)

*Bhor,* blessing, favour

*Bhoráu: á, bhoráu ená, kedái,*° fill up, close up

*Bhorok,* idea, conception, sudden thought

*Bhorsá:ái, bhorsái enái, bhorsá kedeái,*° trust, hope, encourage, comfort

*Bhorsá em,* encourage

*Bhoṭogo: a, bhoṭo: ená,* blow (as flowers), bud

*Bhoṭro,* blunt

*Bhoyono:ái, bhoyon enái, kedeái,* fear

*Bhu:,* hole

*Bhuchung,* ignorant, stupid, dull

*Bhugạ:*, hole, cave of animals

*Bhugạgo: á, bhugạ: ená, kedái*, break through or dọwn, make a hole, pierce

*Ḅhukú*, white ant

*Bhuláu:ái, bhuláu enái, kedeái*,° lead astray

*Bhulkáu: á, bhulkáu ená, kedái*, spring up (fountain), ooze up, gush out, swell (river)

*Bhumbuk*, fountain, strong spring

*Bhumbuko: á, bhumbuk ená, kedái*, spring out (with force), gush forth,

*Bhungráu: á, bhungráu enái, kedeái*, cut into blocks

*Bhụnjáu:ái, bhụnjáu enái, kedeái*, bear, endure, support, pass (time), live

*Bhurạgo:á, bhurạ: ená, kedái*, fill (a vessel by sinking it)

*Bhuṛi:ái, bhuṛí enái, kedeái*, take off (women's clothes)

*Bhuṛujo:ái, bhuṛui: enái, kedeái* take off (men's clothes)

*Bhurká*, morning star

*Bhurní*, small holes in houses for the smoke to escape by; wooden latch of the door

*Bhusku eái, kedeái*, provoke, irritate

*Bhút*,† demon, evil spirit

*Bi:ái, bi enái, kedeái*, be satisfied, full

*Bibák*, all, the whole

*Bibhorom, bibostor*, naked

*Bichạr*,° judgment, thought

*Bi:chạri:*, judge

*Bichárá*, good man, generous

*Bichhíá*, toe ornament

*Bichhláu*, to sprain, be lame

*Bichkát*, hatred

*Bidạ:ái, bidạ enái, kedeái*,° dismiss, depart, take leave

*Bídal*, generation

*Bíḍáu eái, kedái*, tempt, try, test, examine

*Biddáp*, to crawl, walk

*Bidesíá oḍoko:*, go to travel

*Bidhuá*, bastard

*Bidlạio: áko, bidlại enáko, hetkoái*, scatter in all directions

*Bído: á, bít,, ená, kedeái*, bury, embed, insert

*Biḍráu*, to excite mutiny, get up a strike, wander away, migrate

*Biḍrá biḍri:ái, biḍri enái, kedeái*, wander about, be a vagabond

*Bidyá*,† knowledge, learning, sorcery; a game so called

*Bíghá*,† a measure (about one acre)

*Bíghái ái, bíghá kedái*, measure land

*Bigṛá bigṛí*,[O] to confound, confuse

*Bijlí*,† lightning

*Bikol*,[O] uneasy, anxious

*Bilạn, bilạt*, an enclosed plain free from jungle

*Bilbiláu:ái, bilbiláu enái, kedeái*, inspire fear, terrify

*Bili: bálángo: á, báláng ená, kedái*, brandish, glisten, clean clothes

*Bilombo:ái, bilomb enái, kedeái*,† tarry, delay

*Bilṭáu:á, bilṭáu enái, kedeái*, slip away, lose, disappear, mislead, misplace

*Bin*, without

*Bin onmánte*, thoughtlessly, heedlessly

*Bin botorte*, fearlessly

*Bin phasiạṛáte*, unfeignedly

*Bin kahán̠ kahin̠*, causelessly

*Bin hor*, pathless, trackless

*Bin muchạt*, boundless

*Bín sulúk*, unfriendliness

*Bin ghaṭí*, sinless, faultless, innocent

*Bin dagá*, spotless

*Binḍạ*, bundle of grass, &c.

*Binḍạṛo: á, binḍạṛ enái, hedeái*, cast down, turn over, lie flat, fall, overthrow

*Bindhaṛ*, a wooden fence

*Bindi gáná:*, cobweb

*Bindṛángo:ái, bindṛáng enái, kedeái*, slip, fall, sprawl

*Binḍujo:ái, binḍui: ádeái*, sneer at, despise, curl the lip in scorn

*Bing*, serpent, snake

*Bini*, fan (to blow the fire with)

*Binṭhí*, curved knife for vegetables

*Binti ái, ádẹái*,† proclaim, beseech, request, preach, say grace, entreat

*Bio:ái* (see *bi*)

*Bipot*,† loss, misfortune, affliction, injury

*Bir*, jungle, forest

*Bir pakáṛ*, very dense jungle

*Birbáu*, hurricane, tempest, storm

*Bir hoṛ*, wild man, a tribe so called, Sántál gipsies

*Bir jánwar*, wild beast

*Biṛí hoṛ*,[O] convict, prisoner

*Biṛkáu* (see *bhiṛkáu*)

*Birot*,? without understanding

*Bis*,† poison

*Bisbakháno:ái, bakhán kedeái*, abuse

*Bisi*, backbone

*Bisi muṭí*,? unremitting, urgent, diligent

*Bisphoṛá*,† abscess, boil

*Bispíta*,? annoyance

*Bíṭá*,° span

*Biṭhí*, employment for food, work, food for wages

*Bitkil*, cow (female buffalo)

*Biṭolo:ái, bíṭol enái, kedeái*, lose caste, put out of caste

*Bochor*,° year (used with a numeral)

*Boḍá*,* a kind of reptile, brown snake

*Bodá*, ram

*Bodám*,? image

*Boḍe*, muddy, dirty, slime

*Boḍe losot*, thin mud

*Bodháu eái, kedeái*, play to a child, quiet a child

*Bodlá, bodol*,° change

*Bodolo: á, bodol enái, kedeái*, change, exchange

*Bodol hatáu*, take vengeance, revenge

*Bodolachur*, repay, reward

*Bodolte*, instead of

*Bodnám ochoi*,° disgrace, dishonour

*Boḍojo:á, boḍoi: ená, kedái*, wring out

*Boho:*, head

*Boho: khaprí*, skull

*Boho: rukui*, to strike the head

*Boho: kebe: kebe:*, shaking of the head, palsy

*Bohogeái, boho: enái, kedeái*, make a head, put a head on, speak of, abuse

*Bohor bohor*, glutinous, viscous, sticky, thick like jelly

*Boihá*,° brother, relative

*Bojhá*,† load, weight

*Bojo: á, boi: ená, kedái*, draw out, draw sword, drag out, take off (clothes)

*Boká:*, plate made of half a pumpkin

*Bokhár*,† sheath of sword

*Boko*, the heart

*Boko ing, m, t*, my, thy, his, younger brother

*Bokom bahá*,* flowering shrub so named

*Bokṛo:ái, bokṛoi enái, bokṛo kedeái*, tickle

*Bol á*, } *boloi enái, bolo kedeái*,
*Bolo: á*, }
enter, go in

*Boláu:ái, boláu enái, kedeái*, train (animals, &c.)

*Bomál*, to prove

*Bombo*, stupid, dull

*Bon bonte*,? net for fishing

*Bond hoṛ*, prisoner, convict

*Bendo: á, bond enái, hedeái*,[o] close (*e.g.* business, shop), shut up, end, finish

*Bone badári*,[o] highways and bye-ways

*Bongá*, demon, image, idol, ghost

*Bongá soronjám*, offerings

*Bongá burái*, *Bongái*, } perform rites, worship demons

*Bo:ngái:*, worshipper

*Bongá rákáp*, east

*Bongá hásúro:* west

*Bor*, *botor*, fear, danger

*Bor ái*, *Boro:ái*, } *boroi enái*, *boro hedeái*, fear, be terrified

*Borhit*,[o] blessing

*Borlom*,[o] spear, lance

*Boro*, the liver

*Borod,, borod,,,* very cleanly, tidy, neat

*Boroi:*, thin from disease, emaciated, withered; a kind of rice

*Boron*,[o] caste, complexion, colour, features

*Boronj*, perhaps, it might be, rather

*Bostí*,[o] village

*Bosṭo:ái, bosṭoi enái, bosṭo kedeái*,[o] be polluted, contaminated, defiled

*Boṭkoi:*, hill, mount

*Botoro:ái, botor enái, hedeái*, fear, dread, be afraid, alarmed;

*Botoro:i:*, coward

*Botor o:choii:*, an alarmist, frightener

*Buang*, kind of fiddle (made out of a pumpkin)

*Bubrum*, to hatch eggs

*Buchạ: huchạ:*, to snap off at the end

*Buchái á, buchạ hedái*, break off, snap off, nick off

*Budá*, shrubs

*Buḍạgo: á, buḍạ: ená, hedái*, break up (*e.g.*, the floor of a house), penetrate the earth (as a plough)

*Buḍhá*,† old man

*Buḍhí erá*, old woman

*Buḍhá ápu ing, m, t*, my, thy, his, grandfather

*Buḍhí engá ing, m, t*, my, thy, his, grandmother

*Budh*,† intelligence, knowledge

*Budgárí*, wisdom

*Buglí*, bag, purse

*Buḍui: buḍujo: á, buḍui: ená, kedeái*, bubble up; a disease in which the whole body is suddenly covered with spots

*Bugi*, good, nice, well, excellent

*Bugi kathá, bugi juḍa*, good news, Gospel

*Bugi beohár*, good conduct

*Bugi assís*, a blessing

*Bugi sabiṭte, sahintte*, well (*ad.*)

*Bugi ruaṛo:*, to recover from sickness

*Bugi bujháu, baṛái* like, approve of

*Buhel*, to flow, wash away

*Buhídá:*, wave, flowing water

*Bujh*,† understanding

*Bujháu:ái, bujháu enái, kedeái*, understand, discover, find out, comprehend, consider, conceive, experience

*Bujháu ochoi*, explain

*Ing bujháure*, in my opinion

*Bujú bujú*, innumerable, crowds (as ants), many

*Buk áiái, ádeái*, encourage, animate

*Bukạ*, navel

*Buḷáu:ái, buláu enái, kedeái*, seduce, deceive, tempt, mislead

*Bulo:ái, bul enái, kedeái*, be intoxicated, get drunk

*Bulo:i:*, drunkard

*Bulú*, thigh

*Bulú jáng*, thigh bone

*Bulu chirit*,,, groin

*Bulu mayám*, blood pricked from the body to expel evil spirits with

*Bulung*, salt

*Bumbui:*,* a kind of fish [reflect

*Bundis ái, kedeái*, meditate,

*Bunum*, anthill

*Bunum engá*, queen ant

*Bunum baráṛe*,* kind of wasp

*Buráu: á, buráu ená, kedeái*, waste, spend uselessly, injure, squander

*Buṛgí*,* kind of giants who, in ancient days, killed everybody

*Burú*, mountain, hill

*Buru burui ái, buru kedái*, prepare land for sowing by breaking the clods

*Burum ái, enái, kedeái*, lie down (to receive a load as elephants or camels) sit on eggs, lie down in a den

*Busaḡái, busa: enái, kedeái,* hatch eggs

*Busup,* straw

*Búṭ,*† a kind of pea

*Buta,* root

*Butare,* under, at the foot

*Butkí,* yolk of egg

*Buyut,, buyudo:ái, buyut,, enái, kedeái,* throb, pain, tell anxiously

C

*Chá:,* wherefore? why?

*Chabá: á, chabái ená, chabá kedái,* accomplish, fulfil, end, complete, finish, abolish, dispatch

*Chabá maráu:,* die out

*Chábug ái, chábu: kedái,* take up in hand (liquids), put hand into (*e.g.* water to try if it is hot)

*Chábuláu ái, kedeái,* lick, suck

*Cháchárhát,* rough and hard, crisp (as the skin after bathing)

*Cháchásí:,* cultivator, husbandman

*Cháche:ái, cháchoi enái, chácho kedai,* toddle about, walk as a baby

*Chadi,** goat given by bridegroom to bride's friends

*Cháḍo: á, cháḍoi enái, cháḍo kedeái,* dip, bathe, throw upon the water

*Chaḍor badoní,* puppet, small wooden idol

*Chaḍrá,* bald

*Cháechámpá,* original country of the Sántáls

*Chágáṛo: á, chágáṛ ená, kedái,* split off or up

*Chahábo: á, chaháp,, enái, kedeái,* open the mouth, open (as a shell, flower, &c.)

*Chaháu ái, kedái,*° desire

*Chahṭáu:ái, chahṭáu enái,* approach, have access to

*Cháicháite,?* do something irregularly, or by guess

*Chák,* wheel

*Chákdahaṛí,* turban (like that worn by khidmatgars, &c.)

*Cháko: á, chák ená, ádeái,* aim at (with bow or gun)

*Chákhái á, chákhá ená, kedái,*° taste

*Chakí,* kneepan

*Chakledár,* kind of policeman

*Chakmak,*† flint

*Chakṛá,* eunuch

*Chakrí,*† service

*Chál*, frame of roof, roof

*Chaláu: ái chaláu enái, kedeái*, walk, move, go, strain off water, send, sieve, navigate (boat), distribute

*Chalí*,[o] custom, conduct, rites, tradition

*Chál ái, kedái*, hand from one to another, pass, give into hand

*Chalan*,[o] circulation, custom

*Chámá chakar*, a large bird

*Chamár*,† shoemaker

*Chamḍulo: á, chamḍul enái, kedeái*, splash in water

*Chámkáu:ái, chámkáu enái, kedeái*, to start (through fear, &c.)

*Chamkạu:ái, chamkạu enái, kedeái*, to whip, flog

*Chámpá*, a flowering tree

*Chamṭá*, leather rope for cart

*Chámtáhí*, woman with baby but no milk

*Chámuk*,† whip

*Chánḍ*, necessary, fated

*Chándál*,† wicked, villain

*Chánḍo:ái, chánḍ enái, kedeái*, press hard against

*Chándo*, God, the sun or moon, month

*Chándo gáhaná:*, the sun to be eclipsed

*Chándo ránth*, rays of the sun

*Chándoro*, licentious girl

*Chánḍlom, chandbol*, tail (of animals)

*Cháng chungo: á, chung ená, kedái*, finish to the last morsel, take away every scrap

*Changá*, side road, (*verb*) to branch off

*Chánge*,? fresh, active

*Chánghe*, ravenous, preying, (*metaphor*, oppressive)

*Chánghe:*, to lie in ambush, wait

*Chápádo: á, chápát„ ená, kedeái*, toss, cast, throw

*Chapáṛo:ái, chapáṛ enái, kedeái*, be possessed with demons

*Chaple: á, chaple enái, kedeái*, float

*Chápo:ái, chápoi enái, chápo, kedeái*, rest chin on hands, rest the hand (on something), handle, feel

*Chapṛá*, flat, level, even; cockroach

*Chapúa*, Sántál smith's bellows

*Chárá*,† fodder, food

*Charak churuk*, changeable, fickle

*Chárchár*, noise (made by scratching)

*Charcháu: á, charcháu ená, kedái,*° investigate, examine, spread, (as news)

*Cháre:* a straw

*Cháre kisní,** bird (so named)

*Chárit,,,** kind of grass

*Charháu: á, charháu enái, kedeái,*° come up, overcome (as sorrow, &c.) be angry

*Chárháu,* a play at Santal feasts

*Charíjo: á, charí: enái, kedeái,* hack off pieces, graze, just touch, chip off, break off

*Chariodig,,* around, all round, on all sides

*Chárkhá, chárkhí,* spinning wheel

*Charnáu:ái, charnáú enái, kedeái,* flog, whip

*Charpot,* violence, oppression. tyranny, fraudulent, avaricious

*Chás,*° cultivation, agriculture *chás bás,* agriculture

*Cháchási:, chás hor,* cultivator, farmer

*Chás ái, kedái,* cultivate

*Chatía,* disciple, follower, pupil

*Chatkí,* slippers (leather below and rope above)

*Cháto:ái, chátoi enái, cháto kedeái,* swoon, be stunned with fear, start

*Chátog ái, cháto: kedeái,* lick

*Chátom,*° umbrella (of bamboo)

*Chhottor,* umbrella (of cotton)

*Chátrá,* having horns bent down (when one or both horns curve downwards)

*Chhatrí,*† a caste

*Cháuká,?* open place, extended field

*Cháukathá,* shelf

*Cháukáu:ái, cháukáu enái, kedeái,* be terror-stricken, be in consternation

*Chaukidár,*† watchman

*Cháule,*° husked rice (*chánwal*)

*Chaunrí,*† plaited cowtails worn by women on the head, brush made of cow'stail to drive off flies

*Chechlá,* torch of split bamboo

*Ched ái, chet,, kedeái,*° learn, teach; mock, mimic, chaff

*Chechet,, orá:,* school

*Chetis,* learned

*Chepet,, ále, enále,* advise each other, consult, mutually teach

*Chedá:,* why? wherefore?

*Chedá: je*, because
*Cheḍe:*, bald on top of head
*Cheḍir ái, kedái*, have diarrhœa
*Cheḍir bej,,,* vomit and have diarrhœa, as in cholera
*Chedro chedro*, rough, uneven
*Chehará*,[o] nature, disposition, beauty
*Chelá*,† pupil, scholar
*Chelá:ái, chelái enái, chelá kedeái*, be or make disciple
*Cheláng*, pot
*Chelko melko*, wanton (woman,) forward, larky
*Chele*, who? what? what kind? which?
*Chemeng*, mongoose
*Chen̲re*, bird
*Chen̲re chiprut,,,* birds, fowl
*Chepej ái chepe: kedái*, suck, drink in
*Chercheṭe:*, lizard
*Cherej ái, chere: kedeái*, play with a child
*Cheperej*, talk with or amuse children
*Chero bero: áho, bero enáho, kedáko*, chatter (as birds or children)
*Cherká bherká*,? spotted, piebald
*Chero*, a coarse kind of grass used for rope (*juna*)
*Chet*, what? which?
*Chetleká*, how? as
*Chet lagit,,,* why? wherefore?
*Chet chong*, perhaps, who knows?
*Chethon̲*, something, a little
*Chethon̲ báng*, nothing
*Chet lekáná*, what kind? what sort?
*Chet tet,, hon̲*, at all, in the slightest
*Cheṭágo:ái, cheṭá: enái, kedeái*, slap, beat, strike
*Chetán*, top, over
*Chetánre*, upon, on, over
*Chetánte*, upward
*Chetán mohol*, two-storied house
*Cheṭán̲r*, hardhearted, avaricious, miserly
*Chetáu:ái, chetáu enái, kedeái*,[o] regain (one's) senses, recover from drunkenness, become sensible
*Cheṭer dhirí*, thunderbolt
*Cheṭer rŏte*, tree-toad
*Chhaḍáu: á, chhaḍáu enái, kedeái*,[o] leave, omit, forsake, remit, escape, be delivered

*Chhaḍwá*, widower
*Chhaḍwí*, wife deserted by her husband
*Chhai bolai*, collection, all kinds
*Chhailá* chips, shavings, bark (of trees)
*Chhálá*, bullock or horse's saddle
*Chhakáu: á, chhakáu kedái*, strain of water
*Chhále*, cream
*Chhallá badlá*, bullock's load
*Chhamḍá*, a hut, (*i.e.* roof without sides for protection against the sun)
*Chhánchhánáu: á, chhánáu enái, kedeái*, smart, sting
*Chháni: á, chháni ená, kedái*,[o] strain (in a cloth), sieve, catch fish in baskets, &c.
*Chhánkí jál*,? small net
*Chhapkáu:ái, chhapkáu enái, kedeái*, crouch down, lie in wait
*Chhapláu: á, chhapláu enái, kedeái*, inundate, overrun, wash away, overflow, destroy
*Chhápo: á, chháp ena, kedeái*,[o] print, mark, stamp, seal, engrave, tattoo
*Chhaprí*,[o] hut
*Chhaṛ*, enclosure (for oxen), pen, fold
*Chharrá chhiṭṭa*,[o] shot (for gun)
*Chhaṭiạr*, baptism, naming the Sántál children on fifth or seventh day after birth
*Chhaṭká*, gate, door
*Chhatná*,? broad end of bamboo
*Chhaṭpaṭiá*, fickle, unsteady, fidgetty, troublesome
*Chháu chháu*, crowds on crowds
*Chhaute*,? vanish from sight
*Chheilá*, straight, erect, not stooping or bent
*Chheo:ái, chheo enái, kedeái*, bruise, slightly cut, graze
*Chhero:ái, chher enái, kedeái*, melt, dissolve
*Chhilbiláu: áko, chhilbiláu enáko, ketkoái*, jump, frisk about, leap, run about, bustle, be in trepidation
*Chhilkáu: á, chhilkáu ená, kedeái*, heave, spill as water
*Chhín*, appearance, form, shape
*Chhinḍáu: á, chinḍáu ená, kettákoái*, settle (dispute), arbitrate, unravel
*Chhingáu: á, chhingáu enái, kedeái*, stray, wander, separate from home friends or village

*Chhirchhaturo: á, chhatur enáko, kethoái*, scatter, disperse, turn topsy turvy, overturn

*Chhitir bitiro: á, bitir enáko, kethoái*,° scatter, disperse

*Chhiṭkáu: á, chhiṭkáu ená, ádeái*,° sprinkle

*Chhiṭkiṉri:*, switch, rod

*Chhole: á, chhole enái, kedeái*, rebound, glance off, fly off at an angle

*Chhoṭ*, time

*Chhuchhi*, reed

*Chhuṉchhí*,° nipple, teat, breast

*Chhupí*, umbrella-like hat of leaves

*Chhurí*,† knife

*Chhuro:ái, chhur enái, kedeái*, choke, suffocate in eating or drinking

*Chhuṭáu: á, chhuṭáu enái, kedeái*,° be dismissed, obtain leave; be clever, intelligent

*Chhuṭki*, second wife

*Chhuto: á, chhut enái, kedeái*, defile, pollute

*Chhut pheráu*, repurify, perform ceremonies after childbirth or loss of caste

*Chhuṭṭí*, leave, permission, leisure, freedom, deliverance, dismissal

*Chiạ: á, chiái enái, chiạ kedeái*, frequent, investigate, examine, ascertain

*Chiḍir*, have the flux, menses, diarrhœa (see *cheḍir*)

*Chigạri áiái, ádeái*, mock, laugh at

*Chigi:ái, chigi enái*, fall on thorn or spike

*Chiká: á, chikái enái, chiká kedeái*, do, happen

*Chiká chuno: á, chun enái, kedeái*, break in pieces

*Chikáṉr*, clean, white, good (words)

*Chikáṉro: á, chikáṉr enái, kedeái*, polish, smooth, shine, be clean

*Chikáte*, how? why?

*Chikijo: á chiki: enái, kedeái*, slip on the back

*Chiki: te*, backwards

*Chiknạ*, sign

*Chiknoṉ*,† anise seed

*Chilim*,° pipe (for smoking)

*Chin, chinhá*, mark, sign

*Chinkáp*, friend, guest, acquaintance, visitor

*Chinpoṭ* scoundrel, rascal, swindler

*Chinṭ*, paste ; to stick

*Chinṭo: á, chinṭ enái, kedái*, to colour, be spotted

*Chintá*,° thought

*Chipạ, chirit*, tight, narrow, small

*Chír*,° flag, sign, banner, end of turban left hanging

*Chír ḍáng*,° flag-staff

*Chirái ái, enái, chirạ kedeái*, tear, raven

*Chirgálte*, shyly, cautiously, timidly, suspiciously

*Chiribiri*, } spread out, torn in
*Chiribiti*, } pieces, rent in strips

*Chirit* , valley (see *chipạ*)

*Chirit*" *hor*, narrow path, footpath

*Chiṭáṉr*, see *cheṭáṉr*

*Chitiáu: á, chitiáu enáko, ketkoái*, scatter, sow seeds

*Chithkáu*, to sprinkle

*Chitri*, partridge

*Chiṭṭá*, shot

*Chittar kabbar*, spotted, variegated

*Chiṭṭí*, letter

*Choágo: á, choá: enái, kedeái*, nick off, break off, break in two

*Choánṭiá*, passionate, quick tempered

*Chochongo:ái, chochongot*" *enái, kedeái*, sit on haunches

*Chodogoi*,* fish so called

*Choḍor ái, kedái*, make libation, offer drink-offerings, pour out a few drops before drinking

*Chog ái, cho: ádeái*, kiss

*Chogoṛo: ái, chogoṛ enái, kedeái*, be active, expeditious

*Chohonko: á, chohonk enái, kedeái*, dance, or walk, gracefully, adorn, ornament, dress neatly, arch the neck

*Chohonk*, ornament, adorning

*Chohonṭ*, rumour, news, tidings, noise of something, intelligence

*Choilo*, sharp, pointed ; a spike

*Choká:*, *chokla:*, rind, peel, shell of egg ; proud

*Choká: roṛ*, speak irritatingly

*Choká:gi*, angrily, provokingly

*Chokoj*, to wash clothes

*Cholono: á, cholon ená, kedái*,° behave, act, conduct oneself

*Cholon*, currency, custom

*Cholon idí*, be the custom, prevail

*Chondá pŏri*, heap, pile

*Chondái ái, ená, chondá kedái*, heap up, pile up, put one on top of another

*Chong*, (in compos.) perhaps, (indefinite particle)

*Chongá*, pipe (made of bamboo, for distilling liquor)

*Chonrhá: á, chonrkái ená, chonrká hedeái*, seize person or property, put a mark on property, put straw upon a tree in jungle to shew it has been appropriated

*Chopá kuṭạ*, scoundrel, rascal, mischief, oppression, greedy

*Chopłá*, thin-faced, thin, light in the buttocks

*Chopojo:ái, chopoi: enái, kedái*, suck out, smoke (pipe)

*Chopot chopot*, noise as in kneading bread

*Chopot„ chopot„*, low, low spot, cavity in the ground

*Choṛáng*, oblique

*Choṛángo: á, choṛáng ená, kedái*, fly off at an angle, glance off

*Chorchoṭá*, to provoke, speak in dispraise

*Chorhod ái, chorhot„ kedái*, kick, push with foot

*Choro mokoi:*, a kind of vegetable

*Chorpoṭ*, corrupt, treacherous, fraudulent

*Chorṭhá*, villain? impetuous, fiery tempered

*Chorujo: á, chorui: kedái*, put a few grains of rice on the ground before eating as an offering to *Bongá*

*Choṭ*, heaven, firmament, sky, air

*Choṭo*, mouse

*Choṭokte*, quickly, soon

*Chuạ: á, chuại ená, chuạ kedeái*, distil liquor

*Chubạ:*, something small in the eyes (*e.g.* dust, &c.)

*Chuchu:*, the female organ

*Chuglá chuglí, chuglí*, slander

*Chuglí ái, ádeái*, } slander, back-
*Chuglí achur*, } bite

*Chugnui*, to change from blossoms into fruit

*Chúiṇ*,? float of fishing line

*Chuiṇhúr*, sharp, pointed

*Chuiṇyá:*, scales of fish

*Chukạ:*, bottle, small earthen pot

*Chuknrui*, dish of leaves

*Chulhạ*, fireplace

*Chumká: á, chumkái ená*, be collected

*Chumká áto*, compact village (not like the long Sántál villages)

*Chun*,† lime

*Chuno: á, chún ená, kedái*, smear, plaister with lime

*Chund*, musk rat

*Chundui:*, wooden spoon

*Chungur mungur*, fickle, unsteady, coming and going, moving from side to side

*Chupí*, feather in bird's tail, tail of bird

*Chupudo: á, chuput,, ená, kedái*, give by handfuls, hold in fist, take a handful

*Chuput,,*, handful

*Chura*, crest of hill, pinnacle, summit, point

*Churchutui:*, said of children who do not grow either tall or fat

*Churin*,* spirit or apparition of infant who dies before birth

*Churú burú*, brimful

*Churui: cháule*, rice put on ground as an offering to "Bongá"

*Chuţiá*, a small kind of mouse

*Chuţuing muin*, black ant

D

*Dá*, potato, esculent root

*Dá:*, water, rain, climate

*Dág ái, dá: kedái* rain; string a bow

*Dá: irchi*, to sprinkle water

*Dá: árej*, bale out water

*Dá: áting chenre*, water wagtail

*Dá: hásuro:*, stop raining

*Dá: loi*, draw water

*Dá: mándí*, rice water

*Dá: dulí*, midwife

*Dá: tálá ghuţú*, island

*Dá: tetáng*, thirsty

*Dá: sím*, waterfowl

*Dad*, a kind of itch on the hips

*Dan*,* a witch

*Dabáu eái, kedeái*, threaten, forbid, pacify

*Dabáu: á, dabáu enái, kedeái*, overshadow, wear, cover

*Dabí*, agreement; shoulder-blade

*Dabkáu: ái, dabkáu* / *Dabráu: ái, dabráu* } *enái, kedeái*, crouch down

*Dábo: á, dáp,, ená, kedái* / *Dálobo: á, dálop,, ená, kedái*, } thatch, cover with leather

*Dádá ing, m, t,,,* my, thy, his elder brother

*Ḍaḍḍí,* well (in fields, not deep)

*Ḍaḍḍu,* large wooden paddle (to stir up the rice while it is drying)

*Dáḍní,*† advances (of money)

*Dádrám, dárám,* lead or conduct, support, come to meet (used only in compos.)

*Dagá:ái, dagái enái, dagá kedeái,* stop, hinder, cause to stumble, deceive

*Dagá: dagág,,,* jerk, twitch, entrap, ensnare

*Ḍagḍagáu: á, ḍagḍagáu ená,* flourish, be luxuriant (as trees)

*Ḍagmagáu: á, ḍagmagáu enái, kedeái,* rock, shake

*Dágo: á, dág enái, kedeái,*° mark

*Ḍáhár,* road, highway

*Dahaṛí,* turban

*Ḍaháu: á, ḍaháu ená, kedeái,* burn up

*Dáhe,* sour milk

*Dahgí,* household; family, race

*Ḍáhi,* manure heap, manured land

*Ḍahi: á, ḍahi ená, hedái,* blaze

*Dahná,* wages of a servant

*Dahu,** a kind of tree (so named)

*Ḍahúro: á, ḍahúr ená, kedái,* publish a fishing expedition

*Dái,* elder sister

*ájing,* elder sister

*Dahá,* rice (boiled)

*Daháí,* to cook rice

*Da: hái:,* a cook

*Ḍahāṛ ḍokoṛo:ái, ḍokoṛ enái, kedeái,* bound up and down? jolt? walk as a very fat man does, waddle

*Daháu eái, kedeái,* call on, invoke (demons)

*Dákhílo: ái, dákhíl enái, kedeái,*† make over charge, enter, deliver up, give in (rent, &c.)

*Dáldáláu: á, dáldáláu ená, kedeái,* shake, quiver

*Ḍálí,*† basket

*Dalláhí,* slough, mire

*Dál eái, kedeái,* strike, beat

*Dál goi:,* kill by beating

*Dál petej,?* snap at?

*Dálob,* see *dábo:*

*Dámchá:,* woolly haired

*Dámdahe: á, dámdahe enái, hedeái,* spread widely, be notorious, be renowned

*Dámkom,* calf, young ox

*Dám ái kedeái,*° make a bargain, price

*Dán*, gift
*Dán ái, kedái*, give
*Dán águi*, to bring, fetch
*Dánángo: á, dánáng enái, kedeái*, conceal, skulk
*Dánáng peṛá*, Satan, the devil
*Ḍánḍá*, loins, waist
*Dánder*, cave, hole of animal
*Dándhái ái, dándhá kedeái*, think, feel concern (see *dhandhá*)
*Dándí*, restlessness, care, sorrow
*Ḍánḍit*,,, line (of book, &c.), handle (of umbrella, &c.)
*Ḍánḍom*, a fine, handle
*Ḍánḍom eái, kedeái*, to fine, punish by fining
*Dáng*, pole
*Ḍang*, heap
*Ḍangauṛá*, manure heap
*Ḍángrá*, ox, bull
*Ḍángrí*, cow
*Ḍángrí oṛá:*, cowhouse
*Ḍangwá*, unmarried, bachelor, virgin
*Dáṇk*, warmth, heat, flame
*Dá̱nrán ái, kedái*, } walk about, *Dá̱nrán baṛái*, } wander
*Dá̱nre*, dedicated, promised, an animal offered or dedicated to *Bongá*, sacrificial animal

*Ḍánṭáu eái, kedeái*,° improve, amend, rebuke
*Dáṇṭ moṭ*, strong (in legs and arms)
*Dapá dapí*, quarrelsome (woman)
*Dápálo:ái, dápál enái, kedeái*, hide, cover
*Dápálo:*, (mutual form of *dál*) beat mutually, fight, quarrel
*Dáprám*, (mutual form of *dárám*) meet by accident
*Daṛ*, branch
*Daṛ ái, kedái*,° run off, run away
*Dárái kanái*, approach, come near
*Darái bongá*, next month
*Dárám*, approach, come, walk (in compos.)
*Dárám dá:*, bridal ceremony, virgins take water and go out of the village to meet bride and bridegroom
*Dáṛán ái, kedái*, walk, go, travel
*Dáṛán hoṛ*, traveller
*Dáṛáng*, very steep, precipice, steep bank
*Dáráng dáráng*, very hot, blazing
*Darbár ále, kedále*, hold council

*Darbár melá*, court of justice

*Dạrḍáhá*, gormandizer, glutton

*Dáre*, tree, plant

*Dáṛe*, ability, power, strength

*Dáṛe:ái, dáṛe enái, kedeái*, be able, have force, prevail, overcome

*Dáṛe habi:*, up to one's strength, with all one's power

*Dáṛe jokhe:*, health and strength

*Dáreáṇw*,° sea, ocean

*Dáreáfo: á, dáreáf ená, kedái*,° investigate

*Dáṛhá, dáṛhí*, stream, river shut in by a band

*Daṛiạ*, obstinate, stupid, stubborn, thick, coarse

*Dári chhínál*,° prostitute, courtesan, whore

*Darkáddále*, having dishevelled hair

*Darṛáu:ái, darṛáu enái, kedeái*, slip, slide

*Dạrú*, powder, gunpowder

*Daṛup ái, enái, kedeái*, sit, rest

*Daṛupá:*, throne, seat

*Dásáni*, festival so called

*Dasáu:ái, dasáu enái, kedeái*, overthrow, knock down

*Dastúr*,† custom

*Dáthá oṛá:*, kitchen

*Ḍáṭom eái, kedeái*, nip, pinch as lobster

*Dátrom*, sickle

*Ḍáṭṭá*, tooth

*Ḍáṭṭá khorog*,, set teeth on edge

*Ḍáṭṭá uni*, tooth brush

*Dáu*,° opportunity

*Dáu:ái, dáu kedeái*, obtain opportunity, win in a game

*Dáuláu: á, dáuláu ená, kedái*, cut up, mince, carve meat

*Dáurá*, a flat-bottomed basket

*Dáwá*,† to claim

*Dawáṇw*, to wander up and down

*Dayá*,† kindness, mercy, pity, favour, blessing

*Dayáu áiái, dayá enái, kedai*, be kind, shew pity or mercy

*Dayá manáu*, be kind, show pity or mercy

*Dayá mayá*, kindness

*Dayági*, piteously, helplessly,

*Deá*, the back

*Deái ái, deá enái, kedeái*, turn the back

*Deáni:*, security, one who goes bail

*Dej ái, de: kedái*, pluck flowers

*De: chalá:*, ride along, (mount and go)

*Dejo:ái, de: enái, kedeái*, mount, ascend, climb

*Dekhense*, give it!

*Dekhitte*,° knowingly, wittingly, with eyes open

*Deko*, the name given by the Sántáls to Hindoos

*Delábo*, come along (to many)

*Deláng*, come along (to one)

*Ḍelem ḍelem*, slowly, waddling along

*Ḍenḍe*,? bald, featherless

*Ḍenḍká*, featherless, tailless (bird)

*Dene bánáren*, umpire

*Ḍengán ái, ḍengá enái, kedeái*, wear, put on, dress (applied to men)

*Ḍengáná:*, garments, clothes

*Deṛ, depeṛ*, to copulate

*Depeṛá johár*, mutual salutation

*Ḍerá:ái, ḍerái enái, ḍerá kedeái*,† stay, stop, live

*Dereng, diring*, horn

*Desápati*,† ruler

*Des mánjhi*, the officer who oversees half of the Pargánas division

*Dev*, glory, majesty

*Dev lekán*, proud, glorious, haughty

*Dháá*,? weight put into scales to equalize them

*Dhabáu*, to put away (food, &c,)

*Dháchri*, mane (of horses, &c.)

*Dhádráu ái, dhádrá ená, kedái*, rend, tear, drag in pieces, be ragged

*Dhádrá*, full of holes

*Dhákdhák botor*, to be terrified

*Ḍhaká ḍhakí*, *Ḍhaká ḍhoko*, squabble, pushing and pulling

*Ḍhaká bered*, awaken by a push

*Ḍhaká gnur*, push down, cast down

*Ḍhákái ái, ḍhákå kedeái*, push

*Dhakuj*, to squeeze, copulate

*Ḍhál*,† shield

*Ḍhamkáu ái, enái, kedeái*, upbraid, rebuke, succumb

*Ḍhámpá ḍhompo*, rough, uneven, unpolished, knotty (tree)

*Dhandhái ái, enái, dhandhá kedeái*, think of, be anxious for, be absorbed, feel concern

*Dhandhá*, employment

*Dhandhá jong*, be employed

*Ḍhángo: á, ḍháng enái, kedeái*, hinder, be obstructed

*Dhandṛá dhundṛá:ái, dhundṛá enái, kedeái*, bustle about, be in a fuss, make a hubbub, search about

*Dhán rachág,?* snap at

*Dhánso:ái, dháns kedái*, wander over, spread over

*Dhapí*, part of a. fife

*Dhárá*, rule, rite

*Dháráhí*, steep, precipice

*Dhaṛái ái, dhaṛá kedái*, send forth a report, jolt against

*Dhaṛás ái, enái, kedeái*, let go, let fall (as spring, trap, &c.), discharge (gun)

*Dharáu ái, kedái*,[o] owe, borrow

*Ḍharáu ái, kedái*, smelt, cast, water at eyes

*Dháṛdhuṛo: á, dhuṛ enái, kedái*, search, make a noise in trampling

*Dhari:*, until

*Dhársáṉr*, slanting, inclined plane

*Ḍhaṛwạ*, branch (leaves and all)

*Dhasáu: á, dhasáu ená, kedeái*,[o] tumble in, slip into, sink, slip, give way

*Dháu*, time

*Mi: dháu*, &c, once, &c.

*Dhedre*, to become thin or worn out through age

*Dhej*, discreet; complete, perfect; fresh

*Dhejo:ái, dhej enái, kedeái*, spoil? complete, perfect

*Ḍhekáro:ái, ḍhekár enái*, belch, cough out

*Dhelak*,[o] clod of earth

*Ḍhená*, small

*Ḍhenchogo:ái, ḍhencho: enái, kedeái*, be lame

*Ḍhenká*,* "gendaliá" a kind of crane

*Ḍheo*,† wave, billow

*Ḍher*,† many, much

*Ḍhero: á, ḍher ená, kedái*, make addition, add much

*Ḍher din reá*, durable, permanent

*Ḍher idi*, continually increase, be on the increase

*Ḍherá*, hand spindle

*Ḍhere ḍhere*, intently

*Dheyán*, to fast (stay all night on the ground without eating, as Sántáls do before a "porob")

*Dhidrik*, bold, fearless

*Ḍhikele*, rich, wealthy

*Ḍhiláu: á, ḍhiláu enái, kedeái,*° despise, neglect, forsake, let alone, slight, let fall to ruins

*Ḍhilí silí*, laziness, idleness

*Ḍhilwángo:ái, ḍhilwáng enái, kedeái*, suspend or hang by hands

*Ḍhimạli*, idle, lazy

*Dhináng*, then, (future time)

*Ḍhinki*,° machine for cleaning rice

*Dhinkíá*, sportsman, archer

*Dhiṉru:ái, dhiṉru enái, kedeái*, be born, produce, spring, be pregnant, bring forth (young)

*Ḍhíp*,† island, coast, bank, shore

*Dhipáu: á, dhipáu ená, kedái*, heat iron, be eager, earnest

*Dhiráu eái, kedeái*, threaten, swear

*Dhirí*, stone

*Dhirí chaṭání*, rock

*Dhirí káṭkom*, lobster, prawn

*Dhírijo:ái, dhírij enái*, be pleased

*Dhirjáu*,? hush, be silent

*Dhero:*,? be patient

*Dhirong sorongo: á, sorong enái, kedeái*, become weak

*Dhírpúro:ái, dhírpúr enái, kedeái*, be satisfied, full

*Ḍhitháṇw*,° obstinate, sullen, sulky, bold, forward

*Dhobí*, washerman; a caste of cultivators

*Dhobitásá*, a low kind of grass

*Dhodhoro*, hollow, eaten away in the centre

*Dhoká*,† suspicion, suspense, doubt

*Dhokdhokáu:ái, dhokdhok enái, kedeái*, be in suspense, be in trepidation

*Dhompo*, wart in a tree

*Dhon*,° wealth, riches

*Ḍhongá*, boat

*Dhopdhop ái, kedái*, rap, knock at

*Dhorá, dhorági*, assuredly, certainly, doubtless

*Dhoráu*,° to hold fast, maintain, observe

*Dhoro dhoro*, unclean, untidy

*Dhorom*,° religion, righteousness, faithful, just, good, true

*Dhoromo:ái, dhorom enái, kedeái*, perform acts of religion, be true, or good

*Dhorom pustak*, the Bible

*Ḍhuḍhuạ*, small round pot, used for smelting metals

*Dhukáu ái, kedái*, blow bellows

*Dhukdhukáu*, to pant, be in trepidation (see *dhokdhokáu*)

*Ḍhulá*, a shelf, stand

*Ḍhumbágo:ái, ḍhumbá: enái, kedeái*, sleep or sit in a ball

*Dhumdhárkánd*, disorderly, untidy, unclean, out of repair

*Ḍhunḍhá, ḍhunḍhí*, foolish, awkward, dull: large bell hung on cows' necks

*Ḍhunḍháu ái, kedeái*, search, seek

*Dhundhgí*,° dimly

*Dhuṉrá*,° resin

*Dhúp*, two-edged sword

*Dhúp jered*, burn incense

*Dhuṛáṇ dhúp*, burnt-offerings

*Dhuṛí*,° dust

*Dhurun*,? to be dear

*Dhurúp*, flocks, shoals, herds, crowds; name of a tree

*Dhusáu: á, dhusáu enái, kedeái*, upbraid, rebuke, scold, find fault with, reject

*Dhutí:ái, dhutí enái, kedeái*,° dress, put on clothes (men)

*Dhuwáṇ*,† smoke

*Dhuwáṇ rátá*, soot

*Diạṛá*, candlestick

*Dibí*, image, idol

*Díbo:ái, dib enái, kedái*, swear, take oath

*Díb ochoi*, administer oath

*Ḍig ḍig*, bright (as fire), quick (as horse)

*Ḍigáu: á, ḍigáu ená, kedái*, be in vain, be useless

*Digdháu:ái, digdhạ enái, kedeái*, doubt, feel uncertainty

*Digirdigiro: ái, digir enái, kedeái*, beat dusty ground, come quickly, burn brightly

*Digláu:ái, digláu enái, kedeái*, prepare ground for seed? run off, raise the dust

*Ḍih*, village

*Ḍih ghuṭú* site of house or village

*Dihiri*, the person who performs "puja" before a hunt

*Díjo:ái, dí: enái, kedeái*, choke, strangle

*Ḍiká ḍake: á, ḍiká dake enái, kedeái*, shake about, from side to side, roll, waddle

*Díl*,† courage, bravery, courageous, brave

*Díl áiái, enái, ádeái*, encourage, hope, be brave

*Díl báng dharáu*, to despair

*Dúl dálo: á, dál ená, kedái,* rock about, sway, jerk

*Din,*† a day

*Din hilo:, dingi,* daily

*Dinám dinám,* every day

*Din kálom,* last year

*Din machhá,* season, the the proper time

*Din ṭaláu,* spend time

*Ḍinḍá,* site of a house, home

*Ḍingár, ḍingrá,* impoverished, poor

*Ḍing ḍabúr,* to moisten, soak

*Díní,* part of crop given to repay reaper's work

*Dípil ái, kedái,* carry on the head, put on head

*Diṛá mundte,* firmly, earnestly

*Diṛidáng,* swollen (as a corpse)

*Diring, dereng,* horn

*Disại ái, disạ kedeái,* remember, know, be aware, reflect, commend, praise

*Disạ ochoi,* remind

*Disom,* country, kingdom

*Ḍiṭom ái, kedeái,* pinch (as a lobster), bite

*Díuhe,* candlestick, lamp, wick

*Dob eái, kedeái,* forgive, excuse, abolish, kill

*Dobaṭiạ,*° cross roads

*Ḍobog ái, ḍobo: enái, kedeái,* bow the head, stoop, bend

*Dobṛá: á, dobṛá ená, kedeái,* to double a string, clothes, &c,

*Doboṛá,*° double

*Doboṛ,* fold (twofold, threefold, &c.)

*Dochŏt,,* cock's comb (*metaph.* obstacle, *e.g.* an opponent would say, "I have a *dochot,,*")

*Dodorosso,* ill, melancholy, low-spirited

*Dodosi:,* accuser

*Dŏg,* a bud

*Dog eái, do: kedeái,* take by force, save, rescue, wrest off

*Doh,* go away! begone!

*Dohái eái, kedái,* appeal, arrest? attach,? pray, assist, help

*Ḍoho,* tumour, wen, wart in a tree

*Dohoi ái, doho kedeái,* obey, place, set down, put down, take care of, keep

*Do: hoá,:* a case (to put things in)

*Doho gunjáu,* keep back, withhold

*Ḍoká,* a kind of tree, "*jiá*"

*Dol,* a festival

*Dol bahá*, a flower used at the above

*Dolá*, palki

*Dolán*,° temple, big house

*Domáu eái, kedeái*, strike, beat

*Dombo:*, dumpling, cake made of rice

*Dombol ḍombolo: á, ḍombol enái, kedeái*, float

*Ḍombráu:ái, ḍombráu enái*, become thin, fade away; succumb, defeat, subdue; be silent from astonishment

*Ḍomkáu: á, ḍomkáu enái, kedeái*, spread, publish, be renowned

*Dong*, a game (at a wedding)

*Dongeṛ*, a game (at a hunt)

*Dŏno: á, dŏn kedái*, skip, to bound, leap, jump, spring, dance about, hop about

*Ḍorá*,† waist-string, girdle

*Dorbár*,° cause, suit, action at law

*Doṛomo: á, doṛom kedái*, put, place, set down

*Doro soro*, unwell, indisposed, slightly ill, with a cold, low-spirited

*Dos*,† fault, sin

*Doso:ái, dos enái, kedeái*, be condemned, blame, accuse

*Dosár hilo:*, next day

*Dosáu*, to find fault, grumble

*Doyog ái, doyo: enái, kedeái*, be sick, loathe, vomit

*Ḍuḍái*, accusation, calumny

*Ḍuḍurguju:ái, ḍuḍurgui: enái, kedeái*, shiver with cold, tremble, coil up one self through cold

*Duduṛum*, sleepy

*Duduṛumo:ái, duduṛum enái, kedeái*, nod (in sleep)

*Ḍugí: á, ḍugí ená, kedái*, prune a tree, cut the top of a shrub to make it thicker

*Ḍugur ḍugur*, to glare,? walk as a child

*Duhaṛá*, again, once more

*Duhaṛá duhaṛá*, often

*Duháu eái, kedeái*, to milk

*Duing duing bahá*,* a kind of red flower

*Dukh*,† pain, affliction, distress

*Dukhí*, afflicted, distressed

*Dukho:ái, dukh enái, kedeái*, pain, suffer

*Dukhí chárá*, awkward, unfortunate

*Dukh dukhwas*, pain and trouble

*Dulduláu: á, dulduláu ená, kedái*, reverberate, thunder, roar, rumble

*Dullạr*,° love,

*Dullạríyá*, loved, dear

*Dullạr eái, kedeái*, love

*Dulo: á, dul ená, kedái*, pour (water, &c.) cast (metals, &c.)

*Dul perej*, fill up with liquid

*Dumur*, small bee

*Dumur rasá*, honey

*Dundláu: á, dundláu enáko, ketkoái*, spread, (as sponge, bread, &c.,) expand

*Dundu*, owl

*Ḍunḍuk ái, kedái*, to look about at night for something that has been lost, by the aid of a lighted stick, &c.

*Ḍunḍukit*,* a tree (so called)

*Dún dún*, piled up, (*e.g.* hair, &c.) loaded very high (as elephant, &c.)

*Ḍungrí*, hill, knoll

*Dungut*,, *dungut*,, *hoṛ*, crowds

*Dun̲ri*, "*tudi*" eel

*Dúrbín*,† telescope

*Ḍuriạ:ái, ḍuriạ enái, kedeái*, adorn the hair with flowers

*Duríb*, a thing, article

*Durum durum*, crowded, multitudes (especially ants)

*Duṛup ái, enái, kedeái*, sit

*Duṛup achur*, sit in a circle

*Durúso:ái, durús enái, kedeái*,° arrange, adjust, scold

*Dusáu*,° blame, chide, be ashamed, (see *dhusáu*), find fault with (see also *dosáu*)

*Duskụ*,° suffering, affliction, grief

*Dusman*,° enemy

*Dwạr*,° door

*Dwạrí: hoṛ*, doorkeeper

## E

*Ebheno:ái, ebhen enái, kedeái* awake, be awake, arouse

*Eḍhe:*, to sit on one haunch

*Eḍí*,° heel

*Edre:ái, edre enái* / *Endre:ái*, } be angry, scold, murmur, be displeased, abuse

*Edre*, anger, malice

*Edrete* (*adv.*) against, opposed to

*Edre sanging*, to be angry with (*liter.* put one off in anger)

*Eger ái, kedeái,* abuse, scold, quarrel, (applied to women)

*Epeger áling, enáling,* quarrel mutually

*Ehe:?* alas

*Ehe:?* sob, wail

*Eherte,?* command, point out

*Ehobo: á, ehop,, enái, kedeái,* begin, commence

*Ehob* is 'to begin' from the present time

*Etohob,* 'to begin' in the past time

*Ehá jíwí,* desolate, lonely, entirely without relations

*Ekáṛhá,* alone

*Ekkálte,* all at once, straight on end

*Eken, ekenạ́:,* empty, hungry, idle, only, bare

*Eken hoṛmo,* naked

*Ekená: lángtá,* destitute

*Eláng,* splendour, glitter, glory, flame

*Emán, emánten, emánteá,* multitude, of all kinds, collection, assortment, appointment?

*Emánem,?* truant

*Emo:ái, em kedái,* give, bestow

*Emo:i:,* liberal

*Em ḍengái,* assist, pay another's debts (give and put on)

*Em taláu,* help

*En betár,* then, that time (past time)

*En hilo:,* then, that day (past time)

*En párom,* that side, over

*En hoṇ, enkhán,* then even, then indeed, still, *enkhánge,* then, that moment, (past)

*En ḍekhán,* then, in consequence

*En ḍege,* there, that place, yonder

*En rehoṇ, en hoṇ,* nevertheless, still

*En drái,* three days hence

*En derese,* then indeed (in anger)

*Enáng,* then, just now (past time)

*Enḍágái, enḍá: enái, kedeái,* mislead, set astray

*Endre,* scold (see *edre.*)

*Ene:ái, kedái,* dance, play, drill (as soldiers)

*Engá,* dam, mother, female, feminine

*Engá jel,* doe

*Engá hopon* or *hon,* mother and child

*Engá kátup*, thumb, great toe

*Engá payár*, morning

*Engáing, engám, engát*,,, my mother, thy mother, his mother

*Eno:ái, en kedái*, thresh corn, tread out corn

*Epelo: á, epel kedái*, raise, lift up, (*i.e.* hand or stick to strike)

*Epem*, reciprocate, mutually exchange, mutually give, (see *em.*)

*Epem chápáláu*, assist mutually, give and take (from *em* and *chál*)

*Eper áling, enáling*, throw missiles, dust, &c., at each other, quarrel (from *er*)

*Epre: áko, epre enáko, ketkoái*, separate, divide, part asunder

*Erá*, wife

*Erá hopon*, wife and family

*Erá miserá*, sister

*Erándom*, castor-oil plant

*Erbá*, kind of rice

*Ere*, deceitful, false

*Ere yeái, kedeái*, defraud, inveigle, deceive, lead astray, cheat

*Ereror*, to lie, speak falsely

*Ere káthá*, a lie

*Ere idí*, take away something under false pretences

*Ergú*, kind of red field mouse

*Ero: á, er enú, kedái*, sow seed

*Esedo: á, eset*,, *enái, kedeái*, surround, enclose, stop, hinder, shut

*Eset*,, *achur*, hem in

*Esel*, fair, white, light complexioned

*Eser*, be possessed, "jhapna" as *jogis*, seize, catch

*Eskár*, alone, lonely

*Eskár re*, in solitude, alone, privately, separately

*Etá:*, another, different, other, separate

*Etá: then*, in another place, in another's keeping

*Etá: hilo:*, at another time; reverse of fortune?

*Etá: re*, in another place

*Etá: gárte*, re-fashion,? change,? again, once more

*Etá: hor*, } stranger
*Etá: disomi* }

*Etá: mutan, etá: jöntör*, alike, resembling

*Etá: möne*, to think of something else, be absent minded

*Etá: áimái joteko*, commit adultery

*Eṭá: bo: ngái:*, heathen
*Etáng*, slight, thin
*Eṭedo: á, eṭet,, ená, kedeái*, enclose (with thorns), fence
*Eṭet,, achur*, surround
*Eṭet,, achurá:*, fortifications fence
*Ethem ái, kedái*, attract attention by coughing, hem
*Etká*,* a kind of creeper
*Eto*, nevertheless
*Eto:ái, etoi enái, eto kedeái*, instruct(a beginner)train (men or animals) [time), (see *ehop,,*)
*Etohop,,,* beginning (in the past
*Etom*, right hand
*Etomo:ái, etom enái, kedeái*, baulk, be on the right hand
*Ewero: á, ewer enái, kedeái*, to fan, blow

F

*Fasal*,† harvest
*Fakat*,† only
*Fhaḍ*, army
*Fharák*,° different
*Fharáko: á, fharák enái, kedeái*,° separate, go apart, be different
*Fhasád ochoi*,° to slander, backbite, calumniate
*Fhiriád ái, ádeái*,° sue at law

G

*Gábáu ái, ená, kedái*, two sowings of rice, to dye
*Gábe*, marrow
*Gábláí yái, gablá ená, kedái*, tie in a bundle
*Gachháu:ái, gachháu enái, kedeái*, receive, admit, confess
*Gachhí*, sprout, young plant
*Gachhí: á, gachhí ená*, shoot (as a tree), become big enough to transplant (as rice)
*Gaḍ*, concourse, crowd
*Gádá*, heap, pile
*Gádá gud*, confused heap or pile, confused noise
*Gáḍá*, river, stream
*Gaḍái yái, gaḍá ená, kedái*, excavate
*Gádár*, unripe, not yet dried, (*e.g.* grain)
*Gaḍáu: á, gaḍáu ená*,° operate (as medicine), influence, bury in, impress, fix
*Gaḍbaḍáu: á, gaḍbaḍáu ená, ketkoái*,° blunder, confuse
*Gaḍḍi*† throne
*Gadel*, herd, flock, multitude
*Gadhá*,* donkey, ass

*Gáḍhá goḍhá*, rough, coarse work, uneven, unfinished, very big

*Gaḍí*,[o] cart, carriage

*Gaḍí áto*, dense village

*Gaḍí:ái, gaḍí enái, kedeái*, inhabit, dwell, (particularly animals)

*Gádlá:*, excavation, pool, deep pit

*Gadṛá*, coarse, thick (as water when dirty)

*Gadur ái, enái, kedeái*, scratch with nails

*Gádut*, bold, forward

*Gáe*,† cow

*Gáe káṛá* (*káḍá*), flocks, cattle

*Gáe pál*, herds of cows

*Gáe chúr*, a place where there are many paths

*Gág ái, gá: kedái*, weave, spin (as a spider or man)

*Gahánr guhunr ái, kedái*, talk gently, whisper

*Gahí*, decoy, decoy bird

*Gai gám eái, ená, hedeái*, tickle, gently feel, slightly rub

*Gaing guingno:ái, guing enái, kedái*, mutter, talk in a low voice

*Gáịgáịáu: á, gajáu ená*, be heaped together so as to rot, to heat

*Gáják*, dense, thick jingle

*Gájáro:*, to be in difficulty

*Gákhur*, well acquainted, informed, accustomed, clever

*Gáláe*, small grass, quantities of fish

*Gálám gálám*, indistinct

*Gáláng ái, kedái*, braid, weave, plait

*Gáli*, button-hole, loop, loophole

*Galát*,, *soládo:*, to faint? be foolish ?

*Galáu: á, galáu ená, kedái*,[o] fuse (metals), slacken (lime) smelt, melt, adjust (differences)

*Galáu legát*,, *ái*, *legá: kedái*, test metals

*Gálmaráu ái, kedái*, converse, discourse, argue, debate, explain, consult upon

*Gálmaráu*, conversation

*Gám*, story, fable

*Gám gum ái, enái*, lurk about, skulk about

*Gámpátáu:ái, gámpátáu enái*, be sullen, sulky (as one when awaked from sleep)

*Gán*, about, nearly

*Gán*, to copulate

*Gánári*, small fishing net (round)

*Ganbúr*, a big piece of wood with a hole in it to let the water through

*Gandár gundur*, muttering

*Gánde ái, kedái*, cross, lay one on top of another, interrupt, put something to stop the way

*Gandhak*,† brimstone

*Gandhit*, "karait" a small poisonous snake

*Gánḍ garuṛ*, rhinoceros

*Gánḍo*, small wooden stool

*Gangít*,† stones from which lime is made

*Gání sání*, mislaid, uncertainty, forgetfulness

*Ganján*, to crush under foot

*Ganjiạ*, purse, bag for money

*Gáno: á, gán ená, kedái*, concern, be right, satisfy, agree, suffice, hold out, be sufficient

*Gáno: khán*, if, perhaps

*Gáno: dhari:*, until then, until it shall be enough

*Gáṉrá*,* "kachu"

*Gáṉrke* block of wood

*Gáṇṭ*,† joint of tree, knot

*Gápá*, to-morrow

*Gáfilo:ái, gáfil enái, kedeái*,° loiter, be careless

*Gạr*, difficulty, trouble, danger

*Gáráng dá:*, water from a sore, matter

*Gárdí*, clubman

*Gárgádlá*, abundant, ample

*Gárgári*,* white flower, growing amidst rice

*Gargaráu:ái, gargaráu enái, kedái*, gargle, take water into the mouth and eject it on a person as witches do, to oppress

*Gaṛh*,† fort, castle

*Gaṛháu ai, kedái*,° make, fashion, form, conceive in the womb

*Gaṛí*, monkey

*Garí: á, garí enái, kedeái*, brush along before, sweep along before

*Garjáu ái, kedái*, mourn, wail, weep, cry, roar, growl

*Gaṛmág ái, gaṛmá: enái, kedái*, be slow of speech, stammer

*Gároi: sároi:*,? filthy

*Gársílom*, dim, indistinct, unclean, badsighted

*Garúr*, "*gharúr*," adjutant bird

*Gasá gasí:ái, gasí endái*, come in contact, rub against

*Gásgás ái, kedái*, scratch with nails

*Gási*, to fart, make wind

*Gáske*, strainer

*Gásmanḍáu: á, gásmanḍáu kedái*, tread up (as cattle would a road)

*Gáte*, friend, acquaintance, companion; with, in company of

*Gáte:ái, gáte endái, kedeái*, to accompany, associate,

*Gáte gáte*, together

*Gáṭhiá*, stumpy, sturdy

*Gawíj" ái, gawi: kedeái*, beckon (to come)

*Gawi: goḍá eái, kedái*, wink at

*Gáyá*, capon

*Gáyám gáyám*, crawling sensation over the body

*Ged ai, get" endái, kedeái*, cut, sever, pare, scrape

*Get" páṛág*, split in two, halve, cleave

*Geḍe*, duck (tame)

*Gedrá*, Satan

*Gej ái, ge: kedái*, clean rice with hand from the vessel in which it was cooked, stir up in a pot, scrape

*Gejer ái, ená, kedái*, break in pieces

*Gejerá:*, rice broken to pieces, any thing broken up, pieces, crumbs

*Gele*, ears (of dhan, &c.)

*Gele: á, gele ená*, shoot (as dhan)

*Gelej ái, gele: kedái*, dig and carry off, excavate

*Gemeṛ ái, kedái*, carry, bear a load

*Gendṛá*, torn garment, old piece of cloth, rags, bits of clothes

*Genḍwar*, sling

*Gene: gene,?* go in flocks, go in herds, shoals

*Gengáhí*, crooked

*Genthe*, to copulate as dogs

*Ger ái, kedeái*, bite

*Geper*, bite mutually

*Geráng ái, kedái*, gasp, groan (in sickness)

*Ghâne ghâne*, again and again, repeatedly, continually

*Ghangero:ái, ghanger endái*, turn aside from a road

*Ghángŏrá*, a bean

*Ghánṭí*,† small bell

*Gháo*,† a rub, sore

*Ghaṛ*, ambush, a pass, strait

*Ghardí jawágni*, one who pays for his wife by working in his father-in-law's house

*Ghardwárá*,† family

*Ghaṛí*,† hour, clock

*Ghároṇji*,° master and family

*Gharṛí*, ladder

*Gharwá*, sparrow

*Ghás*,† grass

*Ghásí*, grasscutter

*Ghasáu ái, kedeái*, cleanse, scour, scrub

*Ghásráu ái, enái, kedeái*, drag along the ground, haul along

*Ghát*,† ford, landing-place

*Ghát dár*, toll-keeper

*Ghaṭáu: á, ghaṭáu enái, kedái*,° diminish, lessen

*Ghaṭáu gnindá*, just before dawn

*Ghaṭí ái, kedái*,° commit a fault, endure loss, be blameable

*Ghaṭí ená*, it was too little

*Ghaṭí*, sin, crime, fault, sinful

*Ghátí*, clever, cunning

*Ghaunsí eái, kedeái*, to take along with, associate with, take into company or union, &c.

*Gheṇṭ*,† pack, bundle

*Gheṇṭ ái, kedái*, pack, wrap up, tie up

*Gheorá*, whirlpool, eddy

*Gherá*, (a kind of) tambourine

*Gheráu eái, kedeái*,° surround

*Ghiri áiái, ghiriạ kedeái*, revolve, whirl round

*Ghŏnghŏr*, hollow trees

*Ghoṉrá eái, kedeái*, carry a child astride on shoulder

*Ghoráu: á, ghoráu ená, kedái*, mix, dissolve

*Ghoráu mid*,,, mix together

*Ghoṛí*, time (see *ghaṛí*)

*Ghoṛí ghoṛítigi*, in an instant, every moment, immediately, quickly

*Ghor korná*, stores, chattels, effects, property

*Ghulghuláu:ái, ghulghuláu enái, kedeái*, be restless from heat, be very warm, heat (as hay, &c.)

*Ghunghurú*, bells (for the ancles)

*Ghuṉrá*, string of a bow

*Ghunṭí*,° knee

*Ghusáu:ái, ghusáu enái*, avoid meeting, shun

*Ghuṭu*, elevated land, the high land (on which villages are built)

*Gidi,*° eagle, vulture

*Giḍi ái, kedái,*° cast away, throw, put down

*Giḍíá:*, rejected

*Giḍí sái*, throw away, reject

*Gidirá*, child, infant, childhood

*Gidirá pidirá*, children

*Gidirá jong*, to have a family

*Gijiri: á gijiri ená*, be curdled, become sour (as milk)

*Girá*, intelligence, news (particularly of a marriage or death), knot

*Giri*, to cut into logs

*Girjá,*† church, Christian worship

*Giṭa*, string of tongue

*Giti:ái, gití enái*, sleep, lie down

*Giti: i:*, sleeper

*Giti: daṛup* lie with, sleep with (a wife)

*Giti: báṛái*, go to sleep

*Giti: jiráu:*, rest by sleep

*Giti: oṛá:*, bed room, dormitory

*Gitíl*, sand

*Gitíl ái, kedái*, scour, wash, scrub (chiefly vessels)

*Gnám ái, ená, kedeái*, find, obtain, want, seek, receive, acquire, demand, get

*Gnágnámi:*, seeker

*Gnám baṛái ái, kedeái*, wander in search, look about for

*Gnám ruaṛ*, regain, recover

*Gnám gnúm*, to get by asking

*Gnáṉwán ái*, search for, want

*Gnápám áling, en áling*, mutually want, marry against friend's wish, meet, join } mutual form of *gnám*

*Gnápámo: á, gnápám ená*, be fulfilled, accomplished, happen, come to pass } mutual form of *gnám*

*Gnápám gnupum*, twilight

*Gned eái, gnet,, kedeái*, assault, hit, colour, dye, stain, bewitch

*Gneped*, assault mutually, contend, fight

*Gnepe: i:*, assailant

*Gnet,, goi:*, kill

*Gnel ái, ená, kedeái*, see, look

*Gnelo: á, gnel ená,* appear

*Gnelo: habi:,* visible, as far as eye can reach

*Gnel me,* behold, lo

*Gnel hor* } wait, expect
*Gnel dárám* }

*Gnel hayám,* a glimpse

*Gnepel,* have an interview, meet

*Gnel ṭhík,* }
*Gnel oporom,* } recognise
*gnel orom,* }

*Gnel orom,* knowledge

*Gnepel oporomko,* acquaintances

*Gnel gelá:,* to try, test

*Gnel ochoi,* show

*Gnel sahí,* correct

*Gnel baṛái,* search for, look about for

*Gnel saṇwhái,* investigate

*Gnele,* bee

*Gnele rasá,* honey

*Gnindá,* night

*Gnindá bhŏr,* all night

*Gnindá chándo,* moon

*Mi: gnindá,* } all night
*Goṭá gnindá,* }

*Gnindír,* white ant

*Gnir ái, enái, kedái,* escape, fly, flee, run away

*Gnir bŏl kedái,* elope, (a girl going to a man's house)

*Gnir baṛái,* jump about, run about

*Gnir haparáu,* race

*Gnir chalá:* } run off
*Gnir seno·* }

*Gnong,* a little (in compos)

*Gnonhod eái, gnonhot,, kedeái,* to brush slightly against

*Gnúi ái, gnu kedái,* to drink

*Gnúgnúá: ?* a cup

*Gnúgnúi:* a drunkard

*Gnúṇyá,* a drink, potion, cup

*Gnubhuchạr,* very drunken person, habitually drunk

*Gnuṇgnui:* a wet-nurse, suckling

*Gnu áikáu* taste

*Gnukor,* tremulous (referring to the head or body)

*Gnúmo:* see *gnutumo:*

*Gnuṉrá,* hiccup

*Gnuṉrui:,** "*sanári*" a tree

*Gnuro:á, gnur enái, kedeái,* fall, throw down, descend

*Gnutum,* name

*Gnutumte,* by name, concerning

*Gnutumo:* } *ái,* &c., be
*Gnumo:* }

named, famous, be well reported of, be disgraced

*Gnutum dohoi*, to name (a child &c.)

*Gnutum ákán*, renowned, famed

*Gnum en*, named, called

*Gnupum*, to exchange names

*Bahaná gnutum*, the name given to a person afterwards (to distinguish him &c.) [name

*Mul gnutum*, own original

*Gobolo:ái, gobol ená, kedeái*, have authority, have power over, be in power of

*Gochhá yái, kedái*, tie, carry in the bosom

*Gochhá*, cluster, bundle, something wrapped up in corner of the *chaddar*

*Gocho*, moustache, beard; *mangri gocho*, moustache; *sakwá gocho*, whiskers

*God ái, got,, kedái*, pluck, pick fruit flowers, &c,

*Goḍ lagáu*, salute

*Goḍa*, high ground fit for crops other than rice, garden (at some distance from the house)

*Godor*, stout, fat, fat-faced

*Goḍhe eái, kedeái*, fondle, play with (as a child and his mother)

*Godhro*, fat, lazy, thick, (as muddy water)

*Goḍo*, rat

*Godor*, stout, fat

*Gog ái, go: ádeái*, promise, confess, agree, admit, take on shoulder, undertake, acknowledge

*Gogoing, gogom, gogot*, my, thy, his, uncle (father's elder brother)

*Gohá*,° witness

*Gohá gujráu*, bear witness, bear testimony

*Gohanáu eái, kedeái*, search for prey, hunt after

*Gohodom*, stubborn, obstinate

*Gohŏṛ ái, kedeái*, trail, drag

*Gohún*,° wheat

*Goi: hoṛ*, corpse

*Goju: ái, goi: enái, kedeái*, die, expire, kill, slay

*Goj eái, goi: kedeái* kill

*Goi: baṛíjo:* to die

*Gol mirich*,† pepper

*Gol muṛía*,° round (perfectly round, as a ball)

*Gomket*, master of a family

*Gondráu:ái, gondráu enái, kedái*, growl

*Gong eái, kedeái*, give a girl in marriage, answer to a call, respond

*Gongrod,,o:ái, gongrot,, enái* be hoarse (from cold &c.)

*Gono:* custom

*Gonom*, the marriage portion

*Gŏnŏng*, price, money given for a girl at marriage,

*Gonre*, saddle for bullocks &c. panniers, large bundle, name of tree

*Goṛ*, cowhouse, stable

*Goṛi:, guṛi:*, cowdung

*Goṛij ái, goṛi: ená, kedái*, smear, plaster with cowdung

*Goráso:ái, gorás enái, kedeái*, be civil, polite, seek after, keep, support, receive into house

*Gorás sáṇwháṇ*, receive friendlily, take care of, be kind to

*Goṛet*, bailiff who helps to collect rent

*Gorlá*, spotted, piebald,

*Goṛo*, to help, assist

*Goro: goro:* heartily

*Gorob hoṛmo*,° pregnant

*Gŏrŏj*,° necessity, occasion, desire

*Gorojo:ái, goroj enái, kedeái*, love, like

*Goroming*, namesake

*Gosejo:ái, gose: enái, kedeái*, clean the head of vermin

*Goso:á, gosoi ená, goso kedeái*, wither, fade

*Goṭ*, herd, flock

*Goṭá*, all, entire

*Goṭá ṭánḍí*, every place

*Goṭá leg*, complete, finish off

*Gotáu ái, kedái*, fit on (one thing on another), be gathered, confess, adjust, put sword in sheath

*Gŏtŏm*, ghí

*Gotor kathá?* sluggish

*Gŏtoro: á, gŏtor ená, kedái*, run (as fire in a jungle) spread

*Gŏyŏn ái, ená, kedái*, break down standing rice

*Guá*, betel nut

*Guchháu:ái, guchháu enái, kedeái*, destroy, kill

*Guchhí*, bundle

*Guḍguḍáu:ái, guḍguḍáu kedái*, toss about, (as water) roar, thunder

*Guḍṛá* dwarf, short

*Gudrí*, goat-house, sheepfold

*Guḍur guḍuro:* to be nimble, to trip lightly

*Gugui ái, enái, gugu kedeái*, carry on, or suspend from, the shoulder behind

*Guguri*, a small bird

*Guher ái, ádeái*, shout to, call aloud to

*Gulánḍ*, round (but long, as a round stick)

*Gulánj*, a kind of tree with flower white and yellow in centre

*Gulí*,° ball, pill

*Gulíbánṭo: ále, gulíbánṭ kedále*, cast lots

*Gultí?* gossip, prate, tattle

*Gúm ái, kedái*, winnow

*Gumá?* mouldy, dusty

*Gumánte*, according to

*Gumo:?* fade away, dry (as leaves)

*Gunḍí*, cow used to the plough

*Guṇdráu:ái, gundráu kedái*, growl

*Gungú*, hood made of plantain leaves

*Gungudo: áko, gungut" enáko, ketkoái*, to gather under wings (as a hen does)

*Gunhá*,° sin, wickedness

*Guni bhábi:ái, bhábi enái*, be thoughtful, anxious, solicitous

*Gunjráu:ái, gunjráu enái, kedái*, growl, roar, cry out

*Gunsí*, silver &c. chain worn round the waist

*Guntí:ái, guntí enái, kedeái*,° esteem, look upon, deem

*Gupí*, cowherd

*Gupí ái, kedeái*, tend cattle

*Guṛ*, treacle

*Guṛákul*, tobacco (prepared for smoking)

*Gurguṛáu: á, gurguṛáu ená, kedái*, gurgle (as a hukka)

*Gurguráu: á, gurguráu ená, kedeái*, whirl round

*Guríb, guni guríb*,° poor, abject, needy

*Gurláu: á, gurláu ená*, whirl round (as smoke)

*Guro:ái, gur enái, kedeái*, fall

*Gurú*,† charmer, conjuror, teacher, fortune-teller

*Guṛúmo: ái, guṛúm enái*, be silent, remain quiet, cower

*Guṛúm dohoi*, delay, put off

*Gusáu: á, gusáu enái, kedái*, break (covenant, &c.) cross over

*Gustí*, generation

*Guṭek*, many, numerous

*Gutí*, slave, servant man

*Gutiyá*, tribe, relatives (connections who will eat, but not worship, together)

*Gutui ái, ená, gutu kedái*, string beads, flowers, &c., weave, stick on, fix on

*Gutului eái, enái, gutulu kedeái*, tickle

*Gyán*,† knowledge

H

*Hábág ái, kedái*, aim at (with arrow)

*Habbuk ḍabbuk dá:*, wave

*Habbuk dabbuk eái, kedeái*, threaten

*Habi:*, until

*Haburu:*, to eat any thing by jerking into the mouth with open hand

*Hadáb*, to take and eat some and throw away the remainder (*e.g.*, eat the grains and throw away the stalk)

*Háḍáp*,,, to nibble, munch, eat as mice do

*Haḍgár*, a kind of wolf

*Hádhád*, rushing, impetuous (chiefly of water)

*Haḍi:ái, haḍi enái, kedeái*, dislocate neck, put in stocks

*Hados*, to be sorrowful, be sad

*Háemoikát enái, kedeái*, startle

*Hahaṇkár*, barren, sterile, wilderness

*Háháṛá*, miracle

*Háháṛá:ái, háháṛá enái, kedeái*, be amazed, astonished, wonder, admire

*Háhás*, affliction

*Hahí dudí*, oppression

*Háhut*, glutton

*Hai*, woe!

*Hai haio:ái, haihai enái, kedái*, *Hai soe*, } mourn, groan, sob, wail

*Hairá gairá*, to be confounded

*Hájám ái, kedái*,† cheat a creditor, digest

*Hájot*,† prison, confinement for a few days

*Háko*, fish

*Háko íl*, fins

*Hakráu:ái, hakráu enái*, bellow (as a bull), pant

*Háláng ái, kedeái*, choose, gather, select, pick up

*Halái halái hoe*, a storm

*Hálái ái, hálá kedái*, ransom, pay, atone

*Háládwáráu,?* ransom by paying another's debts

*Halbal*, mischievous, naughty, wanderer, vagabond, commotion, excitement [flower

*Hal bahá,** a kind of white

*Háledále*, be astonished, perplexed, in difficulty, in doubt, be homeless, friendless, vagabond

*Hálim,** a tree so called

*Hálo bálo, halbaliá*, restless

*Haloi*, pounce as a hawk

*Hamá hŏmo*, to threaten, rebuke, take by force

*Hámál,*† heavy, pregnant

*Hámálá:*, a burden

*Hámrám*, polished, elegant, clean, tidy

*Háṇ, heṇ*, yes

*Háná, hánáṭá*, that, the furthest, the first named

*Háná purí*, the future world

*Háná sá* } that side
*Háná se:* }

*Hánái:*, that person, the furthest one

*Hándere* } there (far off)
*Hántere,* }

*Hánáte*, thither (far off)

*Háná:*, "mirghi," a kind of fit

*Háná: goju:ái, goi: enái*, to have fits

*Hánḍá*, large earthen jar

*Hánḍí*, the intoxicating liquor made from rice

*Hanhár*, mother-in-law, wife's mother

*Haṇo:ái, haṇ enái, kedeái*, condemn, prove guilty

*Háṉrá hápe:ái, hápe enái, kedeái*; be silent as midnight

*Háṉrobo: á, háṉrop,, enái, kedeái*, catch hold of, catch in a spring

*Háṉru*, large monkey

*Háṇs, háṇsíl*, two birds, male and female, from which, according to the Sántál mythology, all living creatures sprung

*Haṇsí uḍáu,*° sneer, scorn, ridicule

*Haṇsu, haso*, pain

*Haso edingná, hedingná*, pain, hurt

*Hanur jhanur,?* tinkling

*Hápám mundo:* } to sleep together
*Hápám bundo:,* }

*Hápámun*, grown up girl, a girl who has reached maturity

*Hápcháporí*,? clapping of hands

*Hápe:ái, hápe enái, hedeái*, be silent, cease, hush, wait

*Hápe thiro:*, be patient, have patience

*Hápe hápete*, quietly, secretly, privately

*Hápen*, futurity, future (in compos.)

*Háp̣ṛá:*, great, big

*Háp̣ṛámko*, the ancients

*Haptáu áling, enáling*, debate, dispute

*Hápuko:*,* a kind of small bird

*Hạr ái, kedái*, collect, sweep up with the hand, deliver to prison

*Hará:ái, harái enái, hará kedeái*, grow up, increase, become big

*Hará en* / *Hará en buru en* } adolescent, grown up, adult, arrived at manhood

*Háṛám*, old, old age

*Háṛám buḍḍhí*, husband and wife

*Háṛám jokhái*, old age

*Haráṉrá*, gills of a fish

*Harbá*, a small animal so called

*Harchát*,, *hurchot*,,, rough, uneven

*Hárdund*, rebellious, self-willed, violent, obstinate

*Háre pháre*, quickly

*Haṛhát*,,, bitter

*Háṛhát*,, *sisir*, gall

*Haṛí*, put in stocks, fetter, see *haḍí*

*Haṛí biṛí*, prisoner

*Haṛiá gaṛiá*, confounded

*Hariạṛ*, greens, herbs; blue, green

*Hariạro:*, to blossom

*Haṛing*, father-in-law, wife's father

*Hárká*, a covered basket

*Hárkedo:ái, hárket*,, *enái, kedeái*, trouble, be grieved, pained

*Hárket*,,, trouble, annoyance, grief, pain

*Hárono:ái, háron enái*, be perplexed, be in trouble

*Háṛsuṛo: á, háṛsuṛ ená*, get low, (fire, candles, &c.), cease, stop

*Háṛtá*, skin, leather, hide

*Hartáu áiái, hártá ádeái*, serve food

*Háṛubo:ái, háṛup*,, *enái, kedeái*, embrace, seize

*Hápáṛub*, mutually embrace

*Hárub ái, hárup„ kedeái*, cover up, confine, turn over

*Hárum tárum*, in haste

*Has*, pretty, desirable

*Haso:ái, has ená, ádái*, desire, long for

*Hásá*, earth, soil, ground, land

*Hásá leká*, brown

*Hasái khilái*,° mirth and sport, play and fun

*Háso*, pain, (see *hánsu*)

*Háso háron*, pain and suffering

*Hásúro:ái, hásúr enái*, set (as sun or moon), clear off after rain

*Hát*,† market, fair

*Hátá*, fan (for winnowing grain)

*Hatá badi áling, enáling*, vie, contend

*Hátáng*, brains

*Hatáu ái, kedeái*, take

*Hathauri*, hammer

*Háth chutti*,? active

*Háthí*,† elephant

*Háthí sundá*, ivory

*Háthlá:*, armpit

*Hathyar*,° weapons

*Háti*,? importune

*Háting yái, ená, kedeái*, share, distribute, divide

*Háto*,* aunt, father's sister

*Háturáu ái, kedeái*, grope in the dark

*Háubháu*, friendship, mildness, gentleness

*Háuháu ái, kedái*, make a noise

*Haundi*, exacting, exorbitant, violent, oppression

*Háuráu*, to abuse

*Hauwá dukh*,° cholera

*Házíro:ái, házír enái, kedeái*,† attend, be present

*Hedejo: á, hede: ená, kedái*, boil, bubble up

*Heju:ái, he: enái*, come

*Heju: seno:*, come and go, pass by

*He: kedái*, be plucked

*Helá*, timber, wood

*Helá sáhán*, wood for [burning

*Helá helí barái*, be a vagabond, wander about

*Helej„ ái, hele: kedái*, cut, slash

*Hen*, yes

*Heng ái, kedái*, receive, admit, agree, acknowledge, say yes

*Hen huin*, agree together, consent mutually

*Hená*, probably

*Henchong*, perhaps, it may be

*Hende*, black

*Hendeá:*, blackness

*Hendero: á, hender ená, kedeái*, grow dim (*e.g.* eyes by working at night)

*Hendo:?* sit or be idle

*Hendrá*, featherless, with uneven wings

*Henglá*, poor, hungry, dirty

*Henk henkte*, violently (particularly of weeping)

*Henrem*, sweet

*Henremá:* sweetness

*Heo eái, enái, kedeái*, carry on hip, nourish, nurse, bring up children, take in bosom, support

*Heo jong*, have children

*Heo hárub*, nestle, cling to one's mother

*He:oi:, heheoi:*, a nurse

*Hepetáu?* to envy

*Hero:ái, her ená, kedái*, trim a tree, wear away by use (*e.g.* knife, pencil)

*Here*, chaff, husks

*Herel, hepel*, man

*Herel leká*, manfully

*Herhed ái, herhet,, kedái*, weed a garden

*Herhenjáng*, straight tree without low branches (*e.g.* palm)

*Hermedo:ái, hermet,, enái, kedeái*, carry under arm

*Hesá*, "pipal" tree, ficus Indicus

*Hese:ái, kedái*, prune a tree, lop off, cut off branches

*Hesel*, "dha," a tree

*He: setero:*, arrive (see *heju:*)

*Hesráu ái, enái, kedeái*, pant, be out of breath, be parched

*Hetáu ái, kedái*, observe, obey

*Hetet,, ái*, provoke, irritate (apparently there are no past tenses)

*Hetet,, gi*, obstinately

*Hewá:ái, hewái enái, hewá kedeái*, to form habits, be accustomed to

*Hewel, hewer*, bitter

*Hichchha*,° wish

*Hichkáu:ái, hickháu ená, kedeái*, be in perplexity, feel disgust

*Hiláu:ái, hiláu ená, kedeái*,° move

*Hili*, sister-in-law (eldest brother's wife)

*Hing hanu ái, kedái*, neigh

*Hinostá eái, ená, kedeái*, to contemn, despise

*Hinrihi*, tall and slender (like a palm)

*Hipir,** a kind of tree

*Hiqqe:,*° right, due

*Hiráng petáng,* sick man's gait or conduct; dirty vessel

*Hiri eái, kedeái,* visit, go to see

*Hipiri,* visit mutually

*Hiri agui,* visit

*Hirij ái, hiri: ená, kedái,* spill, fall about, be scattered

*Hiri: pasíro:,* fall in all directions

*Hiṛing nái, kedái,* forget, be careless

*Hirkáu áiái, hirkạ ená, kedeái,* hate, be disgusted with, despise

*Hirkạ pirkạ,* contempt

*Hirká:ái, hirkái enái, hirká kedeái,* trust to, hope in

*Hisạb,*° accounts, arithmetic

*Hisạb kitạb,* bills and accounts

*Hisạb ái, kedái,* keep accounts, calculate

*Hiskáu áiái, hiskạ ádeái,* be proud, boast, envy

*Hipiskạ,* to vie, contend mutually, feel rivalry, quarrel

*Hiskạ holong,* pride, conceit, arrogance, envy

*Hissaliá,* slander, backbiting

*Hissi,* a kind of small bird

*Hitáu: á, hitáu enái, kedeái,* be accustomed to (see *hetáu*)

*Hiyạting,* darling

*Hiyạtingno:ái, hiyạting enái,* mourn for

*Ho, hoihoi,* yes, that's true, quite right

*Hoboro:ái, hobor enái, kedeái,* lie or hold in lap

*Hod ái, hot,, kedái,* pluck ears of corn, pull out the grains by running the hand up

*Hodo:,* quickly (in compos)

*Hŏe,* wind, climate

*Hŏe ŏṭángo: á, oṭáng ená, kedái,* blow up by the wind

*Hŏe dá:,* storm

*Hŏe bajáu,* the sound of the wind

*Hŏe edái, ledái,* blow

*Hoho: áiái, ádeái,* call

*Ho: hoi:,* crier

*Hoho sor,*° call to one

*Hoi hoi,* quite right

*Hoi daṛe,* be possible

*Hoing háring,** father in law (wife's father)

*Hokko pokko,* quickly

*Holá*, yesterday
*Holát,,*, razor
*Hŏle?* if then, perhaps, probably
*Hŏle khán?* perhaps (uncertainly)
*Hŏlŏng*, flour, meal
*Hŏlej ái, hŏle: kedái*, pluck ears of corn, nip off
*Hol kálom*, three years ago
*Holong*, flour, meal
*Homoṛ*, to weep, mourn, be sad, be absorbed in
*Homoro: ái, homor enái, kedeái*, be soft, humble, gentle, meek, lowly
*Hoṇ*, even (in compos)
*Honáng*, perhaps, probably
*Hoṇ choṭo*, mouse
*Honḍág*, to stir up while boiling
*Honjángo:ái, honjáng enái, kedeái*, tumble over or into, slip into, roll over or into
*Hopoho*, call mutually (see *hoho*)
*Hŏpŏn*, child, son, young, small
*Hŏpŏno:i:*, pregnant
*Hŏpon erá*, daughter
*Hoputet,,*, dispute
*Hor*, road, path
*Hor udui*, to guide, show the road
*Hor agui*, to make a road
*Hortenko*, passers by, travellers on road
*Hoṛ*, a man, a Sántál
*Hoṛ goi:*, murder
*Hoṛ*, marry a girl to a man
*Hoṛet*, pod
*Horhoi ái, horho kedái*, watch, guard, defend, protect
*Horko jánge*, fence in, keep within an enclosure, guard carefully
*Hoṛmo*, the body
*Hoṛmo berelo:*, bear children
*Hoṛmo: ái, hoṛmoi enái*, be pregnant
*Hoṛo, huṛú*, paddy, rice in fields
*Hŏrŏ*, tortoise
*Hoṛo hoṛo*, man by man, one by one
*Horog,, ái, horo: kedeái*, wear (clothes)
*Hosor giḍí*, have a miscarriage
*Hoṭág ái, hoṭá: kedái*, stir up, rip
*Hoṭá: orej*, tear in pieces, rend (with teeth)

*Hoṭo:*, neck, throat

*Hoṭo: tolá:*, neck tie

*Hoṭor ái, kedeái*, probe a wound, lift up, scrape off, rub away, take out

*Hottete*, on account of, by means of

*Hoyo:ái, hoyoi enái, hoyo kedeái*, shave, peel

*Hoyu: ái, hoi enái, kedái*, be, suffice, become

*Hoyu: ot*, fertile ground

*Hubág ái, hubá: kedái*, chop, split, cut up

*Huchạg ái, huchạ: enái, kedái*, break off (*e.g.* a branch from tree), break (heart, &c.)

*Huḍạ*,° office

*Huḍạí eái, enái, huḍạ kedeái*, send from village to village (the Sántál way of forwarding things)

*Huḍing*, little, small

*Huḍing tárásing*, about five o'clock p.m.

*Huḍing dá: lo ber*, about six p.m.

*Hudís ái, kedái*, plan, invent, think

*Hudís ochoi*, remind

*Huḍu huḍui:*, a little, some

*Huduṛ huduṛ ái, kedái*, thunder

*Hugui: hoe*, light wind

*Huhár*, pigeon

*Huḍhuḍáu: á, huḍáu ená, kedái*, murmur (as water) rumble, rustle, thunder, roar

*Hujúrre*,° apparently

*Hukái*, to snort as a bull

*Húk,, húk,,*, bitterly, violently (as a person weeping)

*Hukum*,† order

*Hukut,, hukut,,* dying? at the last gasp? bitterly (crying)

*Húlo: úle, húl enále, kedále*,° excite mutiny, rebellion

*Huhuli:*, a rebel

*Hulár?* sling

*Hulsing ái, kedái*, sharpen (iron) resharpen, put edge on

*Hunar*,† art

*Hundạṛ*, wolf

*Hundṛáu*, to growl, roar

*Hupkạ*, suddenly, at once (any unbroken event, *e.g.* a storm, a peal of thunder)

*Hupṭi:*, low (people,) humble, inferiors, poor

*Huṛá huṛí*, busybody, pushing person, a pushing and pulling, rapid, ceaselessly

*Hurkạn̲r*,° bolt of door, to bolt

*Huṛu*, rice in field (see *hoṛo*)

*Huṛu huṛui:*, some, a little (see *huḍu huḍui:*)

*Huṛung ái, hedái,* husk (rice)

*Huṛung bhugạg,* break or make a hole (see *bhugạg*)

*Hurut,,,* stump, root (of tree &c. left in the ground)

*Husíd ái,, enái, kedái,* pare

*Husnạk ái, kedái,* ornament, adorn

*Huṭhuṭú,* lofty, high

*Hutum,* to wash mouth

*Hutí,* a small insect bred in rice

*Huṭí,* to become weak

I

*I:,* dung, excrement, rust in iron, refuse of iron, lead, &c.

*Ijo: á, i: ená, kedái,*

*I: jŏng,* go to stool

*I: kund,* hell

*I: oḍok,* refine metals, &c.

*Íạ,* means, device

*Iạte,* by means of, on account of

*Ibíl,* thick, dense (as foliage, *dhán,* &c.)

*Ichạ:* prawn, shrimp

*Ichá: bahá,* a kind of wild flower

*Idi ái, kedeái,* to take away, conduct, lead

*Idi águi,* to bring back, restore

*Idi torái,* carry off, take away

*Idi harái,* carry off some person

*Iḍí,*° ancle, heel (see also *eḍi*)

*Ijárá* landlord

*Ijárdár,* agent, rent collector

*Ikakái ái, ikạ kadái,* leave off, let go

*Ikṛumo:ái, ikṛum enái, kedeái,* kneel, bend the knee

*Íl,* quill, feather

*Ílo: á, íl ená, kedái,* become winged, to feather (arrow, &c.)

*Ilák chhaḍá,*° separate from, leave, part

*Ímboro, boro,* the liver

*Íná:, ínábaṛe, ínáge,* thus much or many, so much, as much as

*Ínáte, ínáteráng* / *Íná mente,* therefore, for this reason

*Íná lehá,* like this

*Indárá kúiṇ,* zigzag steps to a well

*Ingodo: ái, ingot,, enái, hedeái,* bend, stoop

*Ingongte,?* enigmatically, obscurely

*Iṉrijo: á, iṉri: ená, kedái,* extinguish

*Ipíl,* star

*Ír:ái, kedái*, reap
*Íro: jokke:*, harvest time
*Irchí ái, kedeái, ádeái*, sprinkle, spatter
*Isí*, twenty; plough beam
*Isín ái, ená, kedái*,° cook, boil, melt away
*Isiṛ ái, kedái*, grin, smile
*Ishir*, to rub
*Istahár ái, kedái*,° advertise, publish
*Íta*, seed
*Íṭá*,° brick
*Itạt*,,, remnant, leavings
*Ithulát*,? always absent from home
*Itíj*, to pinch
*Ítíl*, lard, grease, fat
*Itkido: ái, itki: enái*, rub the eyes
*Itud eái, kedeái*, paint a girl's forehead (at marriage)

J

*Jáage*, as much as?
*Jábráhí*, handsome, beautiful, middle-height, middle-sized (man or animal)
*Jáegá*,° place
*Jáe koráṛ*,* great grandson
*Jágír*,° land free of rent
*Jáguár eái, kedeái*,° watch
*Jáháṇe*, whoever
*Jáháṇ, jáháṇná, jáháṇge*, whatever
*Jáháṇte, jáháṇre*, anywhere, wherever
*Jáháṇná: te*, in any way
*Jáháṇ kaháṇ*, here and there
*Jáháṇ leká*, like which, how
*Jáháṇ lekáte rehoṇ*, somehow or other
*Jáháṇ tíná:*, as much as
*Jáháṇtís*, whenever, what time
*Jáháṇ hilo:*, whenever, what day
*Jáher thán*, sacred grove near each village
*Jáher erá*, the goddess who lives in the above
*Jáhere*? to court (a woman)
*Jáhíro: á, jáhír ená, kedeái*,° show, publish, expose, make clear, make known
*Jáijug*, eternal
*Jaijulm*,° oppression
*Jájánámi:*° producer, creator
*Jájánámkin*,° parents
*Jál ái, enái, kedeái*, lick with mouth

*Jaládo: á, jalát„ ená, kedeái,* stick, cleave to, adhere

*Jálaní:,* fisherman

*Jalá púrí,* the ocean, sea

*Jalí,* blossom

*Jálo,* a kite, (a bird)

*Jámbe,* jaw, jawbone

*Jámboṛo,** large snake "dhomna"

*Jámin,*† bail, security

*Jamíndár,*† landlord

*Jámká,* tree thick enough to make two ploughs

*Jamkí,* girdle, chain, round the waist

*Ján, ján gurú,* prophet, wise man, magician, sorcerer, revealer of secrets

*Jánámo: ái, jánám enái, kedeái,*° arise, be born, be produced, breed

*Jánám hilo:,* birth-day

*Já: ánámí:,* creator

*Jánám bhŏr,* } all life
*Jánám jug,* } long

*Jáng,* bone

*Jángá,* leg, foot

*Jángá latáro:,* be submissive, subject, be obedient

*Jánge,* rails, fence, slight hedge

*Jánhe,** wild grass, "khodo"

*Jani:,* about, nearly, perhaps

*Jánko: ái, jánk kedái,* be earnest, hearty, strict

*Jánkte,* heartily, strictly, with all the heart or power, necessarily

*Jáṉrí,* hemp

*Jáṉri kichri:,* coarse clothes

*Jánte,* mill stones

*Jánte,** pumpkin

*Jánúm,* thorn

*Jánúm bele,** "bair", a thorny tree, fruit bearing

*Jánwár,*° animal

*Jápágo:ái, jápá: enái, kedeái,* rest on something, lean for support

*Jápíd ái, jápít„ kedái,* close (the eyes)

*Jáput„* rainy season

*Jápud ái, jáput„ kedái,* rain

*Jaṛáu:ái, jaṛáu enái,* be sick, be ill

*Jaṛhí,*° fountain, spring

*Jaṛi ái, kedái,*† fall (as rain)

*Jáṛí,* ? ulcer

*Jaṛmaṛ,* weeds

*Jarndi,* insects (bred in rice)

*Jarŏng jarŏng*, scarlet, very red

*Ját*,† caste

*Jatá:ái, jatá enái, kedeái*, become dirty

*Játá*, sticky, gummy

*Jáṭá*, hair done up in a knot, lock of hair, tuft

*Játur*, skip about (as a bird), hop about

*Jáu hilo:*, continually

*Jáuge*, every day, always

*Jáurá: ále, jáurái enále, jáurá ketkoái*, assemble, collect

*Jáwágno: ái, jáwágn enái, kedeái*, marry, couple, take a husband

*Jáwágni:*, married (man), husband

*Jáwátenkin*, twins

*Je, jemŏn*, that, so that, in order that

*Jedero:ái, jeder enái, kedeái*, warm oneself in sun

*Jel*, meat, deer

*Jelo:*, be refreshed after weariness, grow warm after cold, recover, pull up

*Jeleng*, long, to lengthen, extend

*Jembed ái, jembet„ enái, kedeái*, drink by putting down the mouth, suck

*Jenjle*, beg, importune (as beggars)

*Jenkete*,? virginity

*Jered„ ái, jeret„ enái, kedeái*, burn, light, fire off gun

*Jereṛ ái, ená, kedái*, clean (the floor) smear with earth smoothly

*Jerhe:*, copulate (as dogs)

*Jeṭh hopon*, eldest son

*Jhabráu*, bind round, wrap round

*Jhaiṇyo:ái, jhaiṇ enái, kedeái*, faint, be insensible

*Jhak jhaká:*, brightness, splendour

*Jhál*, warm (as pepper)

*Jhál edingná*, it burns me

*Jhálí, jál*, net, snare

*Jál uḍáu*, trap, snare, ensnare, spread net

*Jhaljhaláu:ái, jhaljhaláu ená, kedeái*, glow, glisten, shine as sun or moon

*Jháp jhápá*, very sleepy, nodding in sleep

*Jhalkáu: á, jhalkáu ená, kedái*, burnish, varnish, polish

*Jháne japáne*, flowery, bearing flowers luxuriantly

*Jhangá*, trousers, pantaloons

*Jhanjhanáu: á, jhanáu ená*, dry (as grain in sun) be crisp (literally, to tinkle)

*Jhanjhát*, very dry, dried up

*Jhánk*, a lever

*Jhanká jhakuro: á, jhakur ená, kedái*, be tangled, be in great confusion, be broken in pieces

*Jhánkár*, a buck

*Jhankaráu*, to complete

*Jhánṭí*,† fence, hedge

*Jhanur jhunur*, tinkling

*Jhaṇwráu: á, jhaṇwráu ená, kedái*, wither away

*Jhárá*, a kind of wild useless rice

*Jharáu: á, jharáu ená, kedái*, repair house, run as a sore

*Jharáu ái, kedái*, notch, pare, scrape

*Jháre eái, kedeái*, extract poison by rubbing, use charms or incantations

*Jhár jhuṛ*, crashing noise

*Jhár jhuṛo: á, jhuṛ ená, kedái*, wave (as corn) shed (as grain)

*Jharkáu: á, jharkáu ená, kedái*, burn

*Jharpá*, splendid (used of trees)

*Jháṭá*, frame for vines

*Jhaṭás ái, ená, kedeái*, beat against (as wind) strike upon

*Jhíj ái, jhi: ená, kedái*, open (door, box, &c.)

*Jhili*, fireplace

*Jhilo:ái, jhiloi ená, jhilo kedái*, hang suspended, swing

*Jhimbiri*, net made of bamboos

*Jhín, jhín báber*, bridle

*Jhinjhináu:ái, jhinjhináu enái, kedeái*, faint (with hunger, &c.)

*Jhink*, porcupine

*Jhink ái, kedái*, strengthen by tying, support by tying, lay in order

*Jhonḍ*, dense jungle

*Jhonk maríá*, of own accord, of itself

*Jhorá koái, ketkoái*, drive along, brush along

*Jhuláu:ái, jhuláu enái, kedeái*, be very ill and weak

*Jhumká*, bells for ancles

*Jhunḍ*, bush, (also *jhonḍ*)

*Jhunko:ái, jhunk enái, kedái*, be brave, mighty, courageous, active, energetic

*Jhunk em*, fight well or bravely

*Jhunur jhunur*, tinkling

*Jhur á, ená, kedái,* choke up, overshadow

*Jhuṭh pus,*[o] false, pretending, simulating

*Jhutiáu eái, kedeái,* catch hold of

*Ji ái, kedái,* smell, snuff

*Jibí, jiwí,* soul, spirit, constitution

*Jiwí jạtí,* all kinds of creatures, living things

*Jiwet,,,* life, alive, living

*Jiwí rárej, kathá,* consolation, comfort, encouragement

*Jiwí judạsi ái, enái, kedeái,* be comforted, consoled

*Jiwí anmanáu,* amuse

*Jiwedo:,* to live

*Jiwet,, dá:,* cold water, running water,

*Jiwet,, hárṭá,* living creatures

*Jiwet,, moto, jiwet,, habi:,* all life long, until death

*Jiwí lo,* to be sorrowful

*Jiwí agui,* take the life of another

*Jiwí gnur,* be disappointed, disheartened

*Jiwí dhirí,* a certain white stone

*Jigirte,* importunately

*Jíhú,** a kind of small bird

*Jiki:,* to walk on all fours

*Jíl,* deer, meat, flesh (see also *jel*)

*Jilpudo:ái, jilput,, enái,* sit helplessly

*Jináu:ái, jináu enái, kedeái,*[o] escape, be victorious

*Jir,** a kind of gum

*Jiráu,* rest

*Jiráu: ái, jiráu enái, kedeái,* to rest

*Jiráu: mahán,* sabbath

*Jirá,*† a spicy seed "jírá"

*Jirit,, jirido: á, jirit,, ahánâ,* glisten, shine

*Jirmogo:ái, jirmo: enái, hedeái,* be disfigured, appear sad, look dejected, be weak from hunger

*Jitạ bhor,*[o] all life long

*Jitáu:ái, jitáu enái, hedeái,*[o] conquer, overcome, win

*Jiwán,*[o] young

*Jo, jos,* fruit

*Jo:á, jo ená, kedái,* bear fruit, be united

*Jo bahá din,* fruit time, harvest time

*Jo bahá:,* to flourish, bear fruit, be prosperous

*Jobáb ái, kedái,*[o] answer for, account for

*Jobḍháu,* to wallow, roll in

*Jobṛá*, chips, parings, filth, atom, mote, dust, shavings

*Jodo: ái, jo: kedái*, obliterate, rub out, wipe

*Jog*,° worthy

*Jog ái, jo: kedái*, sweep, wipe, clean

*Jojo: i:*, sweeper

*Jo: gáṛi:*, preserver, advocate

*Jogáṛte*, carefully

*Jogáṛo: ái, jogáṛ enái, kedeái*, *Jogáu*, } keep safe, take good care of, provide for, watch

*Jog mánjhi*, the person who arranges the marriages of the young

*Joh*, circumstance

*Johá*, cheek

*Johár ái, ádeái*, make obeisance, salute, bow

*Joi ái, en tingná*, aim well, hit mark

*Joj*, great

*Jojáu ái, kedái*, spend (life &c.), live, keep alive

*Jojo*, acid, sour, tamarind, sorrowful

*Jojo rasá*, *Jojo kanji*, } vinegar

*Jojo* ? haughty, proud

*Jo: joháu*, standing ready, prepared

*Jojom*, right hand

*Jojon*, a distance of about thirty-two miles

*Joká*, a worm (in cattle)

*Jokár* ? young

*Jokhá*, occasion, time, opportunity

*Jokhái ái, jokhá kedeái*, compare, match, measure, adjust accounts

*Jŏkŏnŏdo: ái, jŏkŏnot,, enái*, become hungry, wither, get old (as a woman)

*Jŏkhŏn*,° when, at what time

*Jolá*, marsh, lake, "jhíl"

*Jolo:ái, joloi enái, jol kedeái*, blaze or burn, set fire, light, scold, be angry

*Jolo: ángrá, jolo: koilá*, burning coals

*Joloá:*, splendour

*Jol rákáp*, blaze up

*Jolom ái, kedái*, plaster coarsely

*Jom ái, kedeái*, eat, consume, suffer

*Jom god,,* to finish eating

*Jŏmŏk*, crowded

*Jŏmŏk áko, enáko, kethoái*, *Jomkáu*, } dance and play ? (as a crowd), collect in numbers

*Jomot* ? agree

*Jŏndṛá,*[o] maize, "jánerá"

*Jŏne,* wart (on body)

*Jonk,*† leech

*Jono,* broom

*Jŏṇŏ,* servant

*Jopáting,* greens, vegetables

*Jor ái, enái, kedái,*† fight bravely or well, use force, coerce

*Jorwár,*[o] strong, strength

*Jor bajor,*[o] forcibly, violently

*Jorāu: ái, joráu ená, kedeái,*[o] couple, pair, fasten together, yoke

*Joṛháto:ái, joṛhát enái, kedái,*[o] join hands, salute, beseech

*Joṛí,*[o] mate, pair

*Joro: á, joroi enái, joro kedái,* drop (as water in drops), leak, ooze out, shed (as tears)

*Jŏrŏ: ái, jŏrŏ enái, kedeái,* warm self

*Joṛo,* part, share, divide

*Jos ái, kedeái,* aim at, level bow or gun, hit mark

*Josáu: á, josáu enái, kedeái,* injure, hurt, lose

*Jot,*† the whole of one's land

*Jote,* a yoke, the rope on a bull's neck

*Joṭed,, ái, joṭet,, ená, kedeái,* touch

*Joṭij ái, joṭi: enái, kedái,* give more, give again, add

*Jot,, jot,, ái, ená, kedeái,* rub (with oil, water, &c.)

*Jŏto,* all

*joto pakháre,* all round, on every shelf

*Joton eái, kedeái,* keep safely, guard, preserve, protect, help, take good care of

*Jotonte,* carefully, safely

*Jowáu:,* fit, proper, useful, suitable

*Juáb áiái, ádeái,*[o] answer, dismiss

*Juda eái, ená, kedeái,*† separate

*Judi,*[o] if

*Jug,*† ages, perpetual, continual

*Jug sengel,* perpetual fire

*Jug chŏlŏn,* old customs, traditions

*Juhaṛáu: á, juhaṛáu ená, kedái,* get ready, collect together

*Julut,, juludo: ái, julut,, ená, kedeái,* be drowsy, slumber, nod, glimmer, appear (as a little fire)

*Jumáu: á, jumáu ená, ketkoái,* accompany, collect, get ready

*Jungi: ái, jungi ádeái,* be addicted to, be zealous, be fond of, earnest for

*Jupi*, a class of Brahmins who sell beads, &c.

*Juṛáu ái, ená, kedái*, collect, get ready, prepare

*Juṛí*,† companion, comrade, couple, pair, compare, suit, apply

*Juṛí jotá:* } marry
*Juṛí pari:* }

*Jut*, good, ready, repaired

*Jut aikáu*, like

*Jut ámái, ádeái, kedeái*, be kind, repair, mend, improve

*Jutaráu: á, jutaráu ená, kedái*, mend, put in order, repair

*Juṭáu: á, juṭáu ená, ketkoái*,° give, obtain, get, find

*Júti*,† shoes

*Juṭij*, see *joṭij*

*Juwán*,† young

*Juwáu: á, juwáu enái, kedái*, strengthen

## K

*Kabá: habágo:ái, kabá: enái, kedeái*, gallop (as horse)

*Kabá: kobogo: á, kobo: ená, kedái*, hit against, strike against (as a plough on a stone)

*Kabrá*,° piebald

*Kachá kuchạ: á, kuchái ená, kuchạ kedeái*, squash, bruise into a jelly

*Kachahrí*,† court of justice

*Kachní*, petticoat, skirt of clothes, part of *dhoti* which hangs in front

*Kachṛáu eái, enái, kedeái*, dash down, stumble, fall on face

*Kachráu ái, kedái*, cut off (American whitling)

*Káḍá hoḍo eái, kedeái*, stoop, be lame in walking (through an injury to foot), limp

*Kaḍí*, pumpkin; young buffalo (female)

*Kádráu eái, kedeái*; *ái, kanái, ádeái*, be angry, incensed, indignant

*Káenḍe*, unripe

*Káerá*, plantain

*Kafhariáu:ái, kafhariáu enái*, dispute, quarrel

*Kágáṭ*,° paper

*Kahání*,† fable

*Káhílo:*, be emaciated, attacked by illness

*Kahiṉsáu eái, kedeái*, be annoyed, disturbed, vexed, angry

*Káhú*,† crow, raven

*Kahubutte*,* a kind of tree

*Kại ái, kedái*, sin, commit fault

*Kailá*, hour

*Kaingchur*, skin of snake

*Kaingchur lekáná*, fine (as clothes, &c.)

*Kaipí*, an ugly girl

*Káj*,† labour, work, business

*Kajiáṉw*, caution, circumspection

*Káká ing*, *kákám*, *kákát*, uncle (father's younger brother), my, thy, his

*Kákante*, about, concerning

*Kákáti*, wife of father's younger brother

*Kákṛá*, lizard of a large species [woman

*Kálá*, *kálí*, deaf man, deaf

*Kálhuṛí*, young who have left the dam

*Kalí*,† ink

*Kálkáláu eái*, *kedeái*, make a noise, make a row, create disturbance

*Kálom*, next year

*Kálŏṭ*, young hen

*Kámár*, blacksmith

*Kám bhánḍori*,⁰ awkward, lazy, one who spoils work through inattention

*Kámbŏrá*,⁰ blanket

*Kámdá*, to copulate

*Kámí*,⁰ business, labour, work, action

*Kámí eái*, *kedeái*, work, employ labourers

*Kamṉrí*, servant woman

*Kánárí*, arrow head

*Kánḍá*, earthen pot, "gharḁ"

*Kándet,, kándedo: ái*, *kándet,, enái*, *kedeái*, become weak, roll about (as a sick or drunken man)

*Kandhá*, room

*Kándi*, pit of *ḍhenki*, in which rice is pounded

*Kandor*, place of fear, place of terror (*e.g.* some dark spot in the jungle)

*Káne kánete*, repeatedly

*Kánghár*, deadly?, fatal?

*Kangkhá*, rim or mouth of vessel

*Káṉrá*, *káṉrí*, blind man, blind woman

*Káṉrá ghákŏr*,* large fish

*Káṉrbá*, plough handle

*Káṉrbiárá:*,* a kind of fruit or vegetable

*Káṉrchu*, iron spoon

*Kaṉrí eái*, *enái*, *kedeái*, commit (to prison, &c.), deliver over (see also *khaṉri*)

*Káṇt*, earth wall

*Káṇṭá*, throat

*Kanthá*, quilt, pieces of cloth put under a baby

*Kanṭhár*, jack fruit "kaṭhal"
*Kaṉwárite*, earnestly, heartily, diligently
*Kápál*,† forehead, fate
*Kapchí*, scissors, cut with scissors
*Kápelgáe*, wild cow
*Kaphariáu*, quarrel (with words) be contentious (see *hafhariáu*)
*Kápí*, battle-axe
*Kápu*,* a kind of potato
*Káṛú*, *káṛí*, buffalo (male and female)
*Karáhí*, large pot which becomes gradually wider towards the top
*Káráni*,* a kind of tree, "kaim"
*Káṛáng káṛáng*, dense, dark, thick, murky
*Kárár*,† covenant, agreement, arrangement
*Kárár kathá*, agreement
*Kárbár ái, kedái*,† trade
*Kaṛchung*, tall, thin, lanky
*Káṛe*, refuse of plant from which oil has been expressed
*Káṛgo*, attack, oppress, be violent
*Karhạí ái, karhá ená, kedái*, level land after ploughing, harrow (an instrument drawn by oxen and chiefly used in drawing earth to make "bánds")
*Karháṛ*, two bars at entrance of enclosure,
*Karígol*,° workmanship
*Karíndáng*, dense, thick, black (as clouds)
*Kárlá*,* a kind of fruit or vegetable
*Kárnete*, on account of
*Karsáṉr*,* a reedy grass
*Kasá*, unripe, stringent
*Kasáu ái, kedái*,° load, fill (pipe, gun, &c.)
*Kási eái, enái, kedeái*,° castrate (see *khassi*) a wether
*Kasi, kasigele*,* coarse, reedy grass, with white flowers like pampas
*Káskom*, cotton
*Kásmár*,* a kind of tree
*Kásoi ái, ená, kedái*, make folds in cloth, plait
*Kásrá*, itch
*Kastáu: ái, kastáu enái, kedeái*, apologize, express grief, repent
*Kátá*, saw
*Káṭá*, leg
*Kaṭh*,† wood, timber
*Kathá*, a word, order, saying, speech

*Kathá oṛe eái, kedeái*, persuade

*Kathá hátáu ái, kedái*, disprove

*Kathá baḍái*, knowledge, eloquence

*Kathá dá:páli*, conniving at a fault, concealing a crime

*Kathá phạnḍáui:*, one who contradicts both parties

*Kathá seṭer*, give or receive notice

*Katháe*, namely, that is to say, viz.

*Kaṭhináu:ái, kaṭhináu enái, kedeái*, be numbed

*Katí*, a play, round pieces like draughtsmen

*Káṭí:*, small, very small

*Káṭí: táláng*, very small, a little, in the slightest

*Káṭi: chulung*, very little (in degree)

*Káṭ jibá*,[o] be a deadly enemy, feel deadly enmity, be cruel

*Káṭhom*, lobster

*Káto*, knife (of *dom*)

*Kaṭrá kuṭrá*,[o] pieces, chips, break in pieces

*Káṭup*, finger, toe

*Káṭup udug*,,, rebel

*Káucháuṇ eái, enái, kedeái*, be disconcerted, scream, be angry

*Kaulau:ái, kaulau enái, kedeái*, be disturbed, disquieted

*Kaumau:ái, kaumau kedái*, make a noise

*Kauṛi*,† small shell (used for coins)

*Kawar awar*, noise, row

*Káwe:*,* a small red seed "rati"

*Káyán*, sour, cross, crabbed, quick-tempered

*Kazák*,,, strong, earnest, firm

*Kechág ái, kechá: ená, kedeái*, divide eatables, break bread, break up to pieces

*Keched*,? to hit by accident

*Kechel ái, ená, kedái*, separate the broken from the good rice with a fan

*Kecho bedṛo*, chirping of birds

*Kedár*, mark on a woman's forehead

*Kedo: dáká*, supper

*Keing meing*, be quarrelsome, contentious, chattering

*Kehlesedo:ái, kehleset*,, *enái, kedeái*, be confounded, be in terror

*Kelhát*,,, broken pieces, chips (of pottery &c.)

*Kenderpe:*, ugly girl

*Kendri bánám*, a kind of musical instrument made of a pumpkin

*Kenryot*,,, scream of cock

*Keontá*,° boatman, fisherman

*Kere*, a furnace

*Kere: mete: eái, hedeái*, be in pain (as a woman) hold with difficulty

*Kerker*, a stiff neck

*Kerkero:ái, enái, hedeái*, strut about? swell with pride, have a stiff neck

*Kete:*, stiff, hard, firm, covetous, hardhearted, cruel

*Ketel eái, enái, hedeái*, feel sudden fright, startle, start

*Ket hetej eái, kete: enái, hedeái* be insensible (as a dying person), be stiff and cold

*Kewá*, chin

*Khaas*, ringworm

*Khabar*,† tidings, news, intelligence

*Khabelá*, very large field

*Khàchár*, resolute, determined, firm

*Khachla:*, basket

*Khád*, leafless

*Khád*,° manure

*Khádá*, stem of tobacco plant

*Khadbadáu:ái, khadbadáu enái, hedái*, be in suspense, in trepidation, in distress, stick in mud

*Khádle eái, ená, hedeái*, throw into, cast into

*Khadro khodro*, jagged

*Khagáu: á, khagáu enái, hedái*, decrease, diminish, become less

*Khái khabro:*, lament, regret, be sorry for something

*Khái khoi ái, enái*, whisper, be dumb

*Khaiyu:*, pit

*Khajarí*,° rice parched, "*morhá*"

*Khájná*,° rent, tax

*Khájná tahsíl ora:*, collectory, where rents are collected

*Khájná uthán*, collect rent

*Khálai*, grass basket

*Khallá*, plate of leaves

*Khám khuntí*,† post, pillar

*Khámború*, religious teacher, teacher of charms

*Khamcháu eái, enái, hedeái*, snap at, bite, seize by the claws

*Khámdá eái, enái, hedeái*, gambol, sport, a kind of play

*Khámsáu eái, kedeái*, gallop

*Khán*, if (in comp.)

*Khaṇaṣ*, ringworm? a kind of itch on the side

*Kháncha*, cage

*Kháṇḍá*, stick used in sword dance, weapons

*Khándá*, brother in law, (wife's brother)

*Khaṇḍá huṇḍí ái, huṇḍí kedeái*, bruise, beat into pieces

*Khándá purús*, the height of a man with hand raised up

*Khandaṛáng*, gulf, abyss

*Khaṇḍí*, woman's *sárhí*

*Khándlá: khondlo:*, rough, uneven

*Khándo khápuá*, toothless

*Khándrí*, deep, to deepen

*Khangoṭ*, dried up, burnt, parched, (as a desert)

*Khanjáu ái, kedái*, weigh in mind, calculate, ascertain, establish

*Khánjo eái, enái, kedeái*, let down, fall down, slip into

*Khánrí*, cave, cavern, depth, difficulty (see *kánri*)

*Kháp*, steps to mount by, notches

*Kháp kháp*, correct, true, truth

*Kháprá*,† tiles

*Khaṛ*, herd of cattle, flock

*Kháráç ái, khárá: kedái*, spit, have phlegm

*Khárahí*, earthen pot, (see also *karáhí*)

*Kharái*, threshing floor

*Khaṛá: kanái, khaṛá enái, kedeái*,† be ready, be at hand

*Khárang khúcháng*, ill nature, cross, bad tempered

*Khárcháṛí*, cudgel

*Khari hasá*, chalk, (? *karí hasá*)

*Kharíd ái, kedái*,† purchase, buy

*Khárpá*, sandals, shoes

*Khárrá*, salted

*Khársálá*, pure, open, clear

*Khársálá hoṛmo*, fresh, active, cheerful

*Khasá*, brass

*Khatá*, master of a numerous family

*Kháṭár kháṭár ái, kedái*, rap, knock at, gnaw

*Khaṭáu:ái, khaṭáu enái, kedái*, work, labour

*Kháṭí* ? win game or suit, gain

*Khátir ái, enái, kedeái*,† be pleased, agree

*Kháṭo: á, enái, kedái*, come short, fail, be discouraged

*Kháṭo*, deficiency, wanting

*Khátok*,† debtor

*Khaṭpaṭ*, cheat [ing

*Khaṭpaṭí*, tyranny, cheat-

*Khaṭpaṭíá*, fickle, unsteady, mischievous

*Khaṭṭi*, certainly, undoubtedly

*Khaṭṭi ámái, ádeái*, demand,? require? fix, determine, settle

*Khắṭulṭáu ái, kedái*,† upbraid for idleness

*Kháuká*, glutton (man)

*Kháukiyá*, glutton (woman)

*Kháyár* ? gum, catechu

*Kheás* ? mourn, remember the dead, think of sadly

*Kheche: khechej ái, kheche: ená, kedeái*, decapitate, lop off, strike off, (word derived from the sound of cutting)

*Khedo:*, evening meal, supper, (see *kedo:*)

*Khejái ái, khejá ená, kedeái, Khejái bhejái*, } divide fruit or meat &c. for sale

*Kheldu ái, enái, kedeái*,° play

*Kheloro: ái, khelor enái, kedeái*,° perform feats in sport, play with sword, play

*Khemá* ? pleasure

*Khemáu:ái, khemáu kedái*, pass time

*Khemondo:* ? give pleasure

*Khepáu: á, khepáu kedái*, spend (time &c.) beat

*Kheṛkheṛ eái, enái, kedeái*, abuse, (a woman's word) scream of a cock

*Kherwal, kherwar*, ancient name of Sántáls

*Khet*,† field

*Kheṭe kheṭe*, laughter

*Khidi bidi: á, bidi kedeái*, cut into pieces, mince

*Khijúr*,° date tree

*Khikrinri*,* a kind of fox

*Khíl*, ground allowed to be idle

*Khílá*,° wedge, pin, spike, bracelet

*Khír*,† rice boiled in milk, pudding

*Khod*, a kind of tree "jámá"

*Khodá:*, tattoo

*Khode*, grain broken fine

*Khodṛáu ái, kedái*, scrape off

*Khog*,, *ái, kho: enái, kedái*, cough

*Kholáu*, to hollow out, bore

*Kholo*,* a kind of yam

*Khon, khoná:* from

*Khondoro*,* thornbush "kirchichi"

*Khontá*, crowbar

*Kho okhoi ái, okho enái, kedeái*, hiss (as a snake), make

a noise from a concealed spot

*Khorchá*,° cost, expense

*Khorḍá*, lame

*Khorogo:ái, khoro: enái*, set teeth on edge

*Khot*, fertile, fertility

*Khoyo*, hollow

*Khuchí*,? a nail

*Khuchilá*, a kind of fish, "kunchia"

*Khudáu eái, kedeái*, pursue, drive off

*Khukhí*,° womb

*Khulán*, beauty

*Khuláu*,° beautiful, open-faced, to adorn, ornament

*Khún*,† murder, to commit murder

*Khuniáhí*,° murderer

*Khuṇsu: khuṇsugo:ái, khuṇsu: enái, kedeái*, whine, sob, sigh

*Khunṭí*,† post, peg, *sáte: khunṭí*, moderate sized pillar, *mutul khunṭí*, big pillar, anything built up to support a roof

*Khuntut*,,, stump of tree

*Khuṛa*,† hoof, foot

*Khuṛ khuṛí*, litter, palki

*Khusí*,† pleasure

*Khusí ái, enái, kedeái*,† be pleased, content, accept

*Khuṭí ái, ená, kedeái*, give work by job

*Khuṭlái ái, kedái*, shoot an arrow into air, spring up as water, throw up

*Khuttí*, a scrip for journey in which Sántáls carry cooking utensils

*Khuwáu*, to kill

*Kíá*, box for red paint

*Kichír kíchíro: á, kíchír ená, kedái*, boil

*Kichhu*,° some, a little

*Kichrí:*, garment, clothes

*Kichrí*, clothe

*Kiding*, caterpillar

*Kiding káṭkom*, scorpion

*Kiḍong koḍong*,* a kind of wild bird

*Kikiáu ái, kedái*, call out, cry bitterly, scream, make a noise

*Kikir*,* a kind of small red bird

*Kikiṛbing*,* a small water insect

*Kikiṛchi: godo:ái, got,, enái, ocho hedeái*, feel sudden fright, swoon, be numb with fear

*Kil*,† cork, peg

*Kiláu eái, hedeái*, punch? make holes? beat with fist

*Kimin*, daughter-in-law

*Kinbŏkŏrŏdo: kánái, kin bokoro: enái*, abuse, irritate, chatter, continue to talk after a quarrel

*Kinrít*,,, high sounding, creaking (as cart)

*Kiring nái, kedeái*, buy, purchase

*Kiring ákring*, trade, buy and sell

*Kisánr*,[o] rich, wealthy, master, owner, employer

*Kishisáu*, murmur

*Kisni*, "*mainá*," small coloured bird

*Kit*,[*] a kind of animal

*Kitá*, date tree

*Ko:*, crane

*Kobág ái, kobá: ená, kedeái*, notch trees, cut a wound, make gashes (with iron) pat

*Koboj*,[o] possession

*Koboj ái, enái, kedeái*,[o] reclaim, succeed, tame animals

*Kobju*, stooping, bent

*Kochá*, corner, garden

*Kocháu*, accuse falsely

*Kochlono:ái, kochlon enái*,[o] be in pain

*Kŏchŏláu*,? rinse

*Kochoṛ ái, kedái*, hop

*Kod*,[*] a kind of flower

*Kode*,[*] millet "madwa"

*Kodo: kodo:ái, enái, kedeái*, curve the neck, as a sick or injured person

*Koḍor ái, kedái*, clean (rice, &c.) with a fan

*Kohndá*, a kind of fruit or vegetable, "*baitaḍ*"

*Kŏhŏrái eái, kohorá ená, kedeái*, fry

*Koi eái, kedeái*, ask, beg, entreat, pray, importune

*Koilá*,† charcoal, coal

*Kokoli:*, a sender

*Kokombi:ái, enái, kedeái*, have a stiff neck, lie in ambush, crouch down, look sideways without turning the body

*Kokor*,[*] a black bird of night

*Kokoso:ái, kohosoi enái, kokoso kedeái*, sit with clasped arms shivering

*Kokoṭ ái, ená, kedái*, clean land

*Kol*, cuckoo

*Kŏl*,[o] machine

*Kol eái, kedeái*, send, convey

*Koleni:*, messenger, one sent

*Kŏlŏm*,[o] pen

*Kolsá eái, ená, kedái*, push with foot

*Kom,*° deficient

*Komáu: á, komáu enái, kedeái,*° decrease

*Kom idí,*° diminish

*Komboṛo,* a thief

*Komboṛoi ái, komboṛo, kedái,* to steal

*Komkom,* sullen, sulky, have hands on the face in pain

*Konách,*° corner

*Konḍá mánḍe: ái, mánḍe enái, kedeái,* stumble, stagger as as a drunken man, roll from side to side

*Kŏnḍelo: á, konḍel enái, kedeái,* roll, lie down, (see *kunḍel*)

*Konḍhá,* crippled, maimed

*Kŏnḍiá, konṛiá, konḍe: teṛhá,* crooked

*Kondo,* fat

*Koṇgneṇ,* left (hand)

*Konká,* fool, ignorant, mad, stupid

*Konká leká,* foolish, stupid

*Koped ái, kopet,, kedeái,* swell out the cheeks, put something in mouth

*Koṛá gidirá,* boy, *koṛí gidirá,* girl, maiden

*Koṛá jokhai,* childhood

*Koṛám,* breast, udder, nipple, dug, teat

*Koṛám cheṭágo: ái, chetá: enái, kedeái,* beat the breast

*Koṛgá,* blunt, turned edge

*Korkot márá,* peacock

*Kŏrŏi: mŏtŏi:?* be parsimonious, eat or live sparingly

*Koṛṛá,*° whip, scourge

*Kortál,* a kind of cymbal

*Kosolá:ái, kosolái enái, kosolá kedeái,* be in want, be in distress

*Kosṭo,*° affliction, distress

*Kŏtábo: á, kotáp,, enái, kedeái,* rap (with a stick or finger)

*Koṭágo: á, koṭá: enái, kedeái,* shake (clothes, feet, &c.)

*Koṭá: giḍí,* shake off, shake up and throw away the bad

*Koṭejo: ái, koṭe: enái, kedeái,* beat (with a stone or fist), bruise up

*Koṭhá oṛá:,* two storied house, roof

*Kothráo: á, kothrá enái, kedeái,* be injured, suffer loss

*Koṭo,* naked

*Kowále,* beam, rafter

*Koyog,,o: ái, koyo: enái, kedeái,* await, gaze anxiously, expect, look up, stare, glance

*Koyu,* mango stone

*Krús,*† cross

*Kuchilá,** a kind of tree

*Kuḍámrenko,* neighbour's

*Kudáu eái, kedeái,* chase, persecute, pursue, follow (see *khudáu*)

*Kuḍí,°* a kind of hoe

*Kuḍu,* boar

*Kudum,* riddle, enigma

*Kuduṛ huduṛo:ái, kuduṛ enái, kedeái,* be nimble, tripping (as a woman) walk lively

*Kuhaṛá,°* dust, fog, mist

*Kuháu ái, enái, kedeái,* strike with fist

*Kuhnráu:ái, kuhnráu enái, kedái,* sob, cry

*Kuilí,* a peg (of wood) wedge

*Kuíṇ,†* a well

*Kuinḍi,** a tree "mhowá", see also *máthom*

*Kujiri,** a kind of tree

*Kukár* ? smear with cow dung

*Kukhí,°* womb (see *khukhí*)

*Kukmú,* a dream

*Kukmu: ái, kukmu kedái,* dream

*Kukṛuchu:,* cockscomb

*Kukṛuchug ái, kukruchu: kedái,* crow, (as a cock)

*Kukujo: ái, kukui: enái, kedeái,* sleep with arms and legs folded in a ball, bend arm or leg

*Kukuká,* raise one corner of mat and cover the rice which is drying on it

*Kukunáu:ái, kukunáu enái, kedái,* hold urine till it is painful

*Kukuhu,* singing of a dove

*Kukute* ? plaything

*Kukut,, kuḳut,,* ? dying, at point of death

*Kul, kul erá,* tiger, tigress

*Kulai,* hare, rabbit

*Kuláu ái, enái, kedeái,* supply, make up deficit

*Kulhí,* street of a village

*Kulhí daṛup,* assembly, meeting, *panchayat*

*Kulhí muchạt,,,* just outside the village

*Kuli eái, kedeái,* ask, inquire, request

*Kulkhí,* dark or secret chamber

*Kulsuring,* poisonous lizard

*Kulup,* lock, padlock

*Kulup káṭhí,* key

*Kúm,* leathern bags in which the Mahajans carry oil

*Kumá ing, m, t,* my, thy, his uncle (father's sister's husband)

*Kumáu:,°* want, (see *komáu*)

*Kumbá,* hut made of sticks,

place like an inverted V in form, shed

*Kumburu ái, kedeái*, rob, steal

*Kukumburu: i:*, robber, thief

*Kumburu orá:*, prison

*Kumí*,° want, be deficient

*Kumtí idí:*° decrease, diminish

*Kunám*,* a kind of tree

*Kunámí*, half moon

*Kundáu: á, kundáu ená, kedái*, compose, make, engrave, carve out, fashion, turn in lathe

*Kundel*, roll (see *kondel*)

*Kunduri, kunám*, a wild fruit

*Kundhí*, kidney of chicken

*Kungkál*, wasp, potter

*Kunhráu:ái, kunhráu kedái*, groan (in sickness)

*Kunkunáu:ái, kunkunáu enái*, quarrel, be angry

*Kupí*, earthen oil-can, vessel with small mouth

*Kupuli áling, enáling*, converse, ask and answer

*Kuputiyá*,° hypocritical

*Kurá gidirá*, boy, *kurí gidirá*, girl, (see *korá, korí*)

*Kurai*, wages

*Kurámre kudámre*, behind (place)

*Kuráu: á, kuráu ená, kedái*, suit, answer the purpose, suffice, be wanting, be deficient, be unable, be unfinished, be collected

*Kurchungo:ái, kurchung enái, kedeái*, limp (as dog) bend the knee (as a sleeping person)

*Kurhiyá*, lazy, idle

*Kurit rámá*, thornbush, "*kánákol*"

*Kuríyá*, hut

*Kurkundui:*, staringly

*Kuromutáhá*, disobliging, morose, unsocial

*Kurum*, sound of musical instrument, small drum

*Kurumutu:ái, kurumutui enái kurumutu kedái*, be active, energetic, attend diligently

*Kurumutute*, diligently, actively, earnestly

*Kusbí*,° prostitute, whore

*Kusbí bahá*, a kind of flower

*Kustá*, chaff

*Kusu: kusudo:ái, kusut,, enái, kedeái*, whine, sob, sigh, sniffle (see *khunsu:*)

*Kutám eái, enái, kedeái*, to hammer, make holes, strike with axe, hoe, &c., pierce, punch

*Kutám bid,,*, drive in (a nail, &c.)

*Kuṭám ḍángrá*, sacrificial bullock

*Kuṭásí*, hammer

*Kuṭburo:ái, kuṭbur enái, kedeái*, sit with head between the knees

*Kuṭhánr*, dry pieces of ground in wet fields or road, &c.

*Kuṭhe*, leg (of chair, table)

*Kuṭhí*,° storehouse

*Kuṭhíl*, miserly, unmerciful (only of women)

*Kuṭí ái, ákádái*, cut up, mince (meat, vegetables)

*Kuṭkuṭu:ái, kuṭkuṭui enái, kutkuṭu kedeái*, raise the back (as a cat)

*Kuṭrạ eái, enái, kedeái*, break in pieces

*Kuṭrạ*, a piece

*Kyonṭá*,° fisherman

## L

*Láb, lábh*,† gain, profit

*Láb ái, kedái*, gain, profit

*Láb ochoi*, make profitable, useful

*Lábáṛ*, false, untrue

*Lábi:*, soft, mild, pliable, tender

*Lábido: á, lábit„ ená, kedeái*, become soft, melt a person by entreaty

*Láchár*,† distressed, helpless

*Lád ái, lát„ kedái*, roast meat, bind meat, &c. in leaves

*Láde eái, ená, kedeái*, bend, load, put over, put one thing on another, fall upon, spring upon

*Láde jong*, put on (as clothes)

*Ladeá*, crooked tree

*Lád lád*, crowds on crowds, gelatinous, thick

*Láḍu*, a kind of sweetmeat

*Lág ái, lá: kedái*, shave timber, chip wood

*Lá: gulánḍ*, round timber

*Lagá eái, kedeái*, pursue, drive off, chase

*Lagá gnir*, drive off or away

*Lagá lagí*, one after another, close together

*Lagám*,° saddle

*Lagan bagan*, trade, traffic

*Lágáu ái, ená, kedeái*, apply, begin, contend, vie

*Lagít, lagát„*, for, on account of

*Lág lág* chips, wood

*Lágonre*, a kind of bird

*Lahá:ái, laháі enái, lahá kedeái*, guide, send on in front, go in front

*Lahánto: ái, lahá: enái, kedeái*, beat, excel, surpass, guide, go in front, send on

*Laháte*, in front, to the front

*Lahúse:*, in front of, before, in presence of

*Laháreá kathá*, prophecy

*Lahár chahár*, ostentation, display

*Láhárá*, flying clouds

*Lại eái, ádeái*, speak, tell, (*dat.*) tell tales of another, say, describe, direct, mention, (*acc.*)

*Lại ocho*, dictate

*Lại báṛái*, mention

*Lại lábáṛ*, liar

*Lại ṭhík*, arrange, settle

*Lái:*, belly, womb, bowels, entrails

*Lái: oḍoko: ái, oḍok enái*, have diarrhœa

*Láijo: ái, lái: enái*, be pregnant

*Lái: látáro:*, be submissive, obedient

*Lái: tuliáu:* fill the belly, satisfy

*Lái ái, lá kedái*, dig

*Lá ṭánḍí*, dig up

*Lajáu: ái, lajáu enái, kedeái*,[o] feel shame, be diffident

*Lakáṛ lukuṛo:ái, lukuṛ enái, kedeái*, shake from side to side, waddle, shake in the legs, tremble, be weak in feet

*Lákuj ái, lákui: enái, kedeái, or ádeái*, bend over, hang down

*Lalá:ái, kedái,* / *Lá: ái, &c.* } chip, smooth, scrape

*Laláu:*, to suffer (pain, hunger, &c.)

*Láloch*,† avarice

*Lálocho:ái, láloch enái, kedeái*, covet, crave, long for

*Lái lukṭhá:ái, lukṭhái enái, lukṭhá kedeái*, contend with, pick quarrel with, annoy

*Lámá:*,* a kind of flower

*Lámbáu: á, lámbáu ená, kedái*, decay, become stale

*Lámbe*, 2nd crop growing of itself

*Lámkám*, idle

*Lámpoṭ*, buffoon

*Lándái ái, lándá kedái*, laugh

*Lándái*, joke

*Lá: ndái:*, joker

*Lándái leká*, absurd

*Landhu ái, ená, kedái*, infringe, break (order, covenant, &c.) press down, (crops, &c.) be violent, tread down

*Lándŏr dhing*, arrived at manhood

*Lánduro: á, lándur ená, kedái*, raze, demolish, tumble down

*Lángá*, weary

*Lángá:ái, lángái enái, lángá kedái*, be weary

*Lángtá*, naked, destitute, poor

*Láng titi*,* a small long-tailed bird

*Lápá: chápá: á, chápái enái, chápá kedái*, fall to pieces

*Lapai*, converse, talk together

*Lapa lopo* fly as young birds

*Láped„ ái, lápet„ kedái*, eat by morsels, take a mouthful

*Láphuá*, ridiculous, ludicrous, foolish

*Lápichkká:*, corpulent woman

*Lápít*, barber (Hindu)

*Láp lápá ái, ená kedeái*, spread open (as a book, paper, cloth, &c.)

*Lár*, a creeper, any thing pliant, a slender snake

*Lárău: á, lárău ená, kedeái*, quake, shake, move the lips quickly, work

*Larhái ái, enáling*,† to fight, contend

*Lárká*, the Coles

*Larkharău:ái, larkharău enái, kedái*, speak fast, wish to get out words, run round and round (*e.g.*, animal in cage)

*Lárkujo: á, lárkui: ená, kedái*, bend a tree to get the fruit (see *lákuj„*)

*Láserá:*, sharp, pointed

*Lásero: á, láser ená, kedái*, sharpen iron, to talk fluently (as a drunken man)

*Láshár*,† sailor

*Látárre, látárte*, under, beneath

*Látghát*, commit fornication, copulate

*Lathá*, birdlime

*Láthe*, a kind of fruit-tree

*Látíjo:ái, láti: kedái*, bend the body back by shoulders so as to make the chest protrude

*Latpat*, roll (in the mud, &c.)

*Látpatău*,° faint (from hunger, sickness, &c.)

*Lấtu látu*, round (as fruit)

*Látum ái, kedái*, devour, swallow up greedily

*Láṭumo:ái, láṭum ená, kedái*, seize, double, fold up

*Lauka*,[o] boat

*Láuṭá*, snare for birds

*Láwero:ái, láwer ená, kedeái*, bend, incline

*Leá ená, kedái*, wash away as by a flood, crumble away, melt, dissolve, fall to dust or powder

*Leáu*, play, sport

*Lebdái ái, lebdá kedeái*, cast (a net), throw, throw away

*Lebedo:ái, lebet,, kedeái*, kick, press down

*Le: bedá gándo*, footstool

*Lebet,, gásmándáu: á, gásmándáu ená, kedeái*, tread under foot

*Lebṛá*, glutton, covetous

*Leche leche*,? unequal? uneven? unsteady, as a man carrying a heavy weight

*Lechej,, ái, leche: enái, kedái*, winnow, throw up grain in fan to sift it

*Ledám*,? edge

*Leḍhá:ái, leḍhái enái, leḍhá kedeái*, be lame, limp

*Leḍhí*, lame (woman)

*Leg*, fit, suitable, proper, custom, right, due

*Lego:ái, leg kedái*, act properly, act according to custom

*Lege: lábágo: á, lábá: ená, kedái*, be tender, be verdant, be soft (as grass)

*Lege: lege:*, tender, green, &c. (grass)

*Lege: legejo: á, lege: enái, kedái*, be green, be flourishing

*Legem legem*, softly, gently

*Legesá:*, fat, plump (as children)

*Lek*,[o] worthy

*Lekte*,[o] worthily

*Leká*, like

*Leká ái, kedái*, liken

*Lekhái ái, ená, kedeái*,[o] count, reckon, esteem, deem, add up, consider, resemble

*Lekhá jokhái*,[o] keep accounts

*Lekhá*,[o] a number

*Lelhá, lelhí*, foolish (man, woman) blockhead, dunce

*Lelenge:*, smooth, placid, distant object, indistinct

*Lemeng*, powder

*Lemeng lemeng nái, ená, kedái*, pulverize

*Lemlem*, gently, gracefully

*Lemṭo:*, unripe, tasteless

*Len ái, ená, kedeái*, squeeze out, express (oil, &c.), press

*Leno: páṭá* oil press

*Lendá*, sediment, dregs, very small

*Lenḍe:*, earthworm

*Lende mochá:*,? nearly ripe

*Lengá*, left hand or foot

*Leng chalá:*, crawl along (as a snake)

*Lenge: lengedo: ái, lenget,, enái kedeái*, be in danger

*Lengnedo:* }
*Lenjedo:ái, lenjet,,* } slip, slide
*enái, kedeái,* }

*Lenjer, lenjet*, slippery, greasy, polished, muddy

*Leohái ái, ená, kedái*, mix, stir up

*Lepen tepen*, piled up, irregular, rabble, crowd

*Leper leper*, paste, starch, mud and water

*Lepe: teṛel*, a kind of tree "kendu"

*Lere*,? expedient, plan, means

*Lesáṉrhe:*, to come with false pretences

*Lesej,, ái, lese: kedeái*, snap, snarl

*Lesen*, to knock over by foot

*Lese pese: á, lese pese ená, kedái*, make mud, become muddy

*Lesker*, fat (as pigs)

*Letej ái, lete: kedái*, accomplish purpose, perform successfully

*Leṭep,, leṭep,,*, lifeless, half dead

*Leṭe peṭe*, mudlike, rice cooked into a paste

*Lethá*,? children

*Libir libir*, soft, flabby as earth after rain, or leather when wet

*Lichạr*,[O] weak, helpless

*Likit,, likido: á, likit,, ená, kedái*, swing in the wind, shake about (as branch)

*Lál*,[O] indigo

*Lálám*,[O] a sale, auction

*Lálámo:*, have a sale or auction

*Limbodo:ái, limbot,, ená, kedeái*, strangle, be strangled

*Lin ái, kedeái*, pinch, catch tight, hold by a gripe

*Linḍạro: ái, linḍạr enái, kedeái*, attend to business, be skilful, clever, be well accquainted with

*Lindi*, fundament

*Lindi eái, kedeái,* mock

*Linjido: á, linjit,, ená, kedái,* flow in drops, run gently, trickle

*Lipi,** a kind of small bird

*Lipindhi,* glistening, shining, glittering, as crystal

*Lip lip,* clear, transparent, burnished

*Lipsá,* limber, pliant

*Lipúr lipúr,* tinkling, a jingling instrument bound on hands, feet or wrist

*Liṛi:,* child, small

*Liṛi: gidirá,* baby

*Lisind ái, kedái,* hunt for a fault, seek occasion against, exaggerate evil

*Liṭạ,* rainbow

*Liṭi:,* to decay, become bad, (as meat, rice, &c.), rot

*Liwá liwi:,* to bob about

*Liwedo: á, liwet,, enái, kedeái,* bend down

*Lo:ái, lo ená, kedái,* burn

*Lobdháu:ái, lobdháu enái, kedeái,* be surprised, charmed, delighted

*Lobh ái, kedái,*° covet

*Lobhátíyá,?* covetous

*Lobháu eái, enái, kedeái,* seduce, amuse, divert

*Lobo: lobo:,?* jolt? jerk? stout

*Lobo: muiṇ,* red ant (very small)

*Lochái ái, lochá kedái,* eat (with hands) put hand into dish

*Lopochá,* eat together off one plate

*Lo dá:, su: dá:,* well, a small hole in sand near a river

*Lodám,* a kind of tree, first step on a hill, rising ground at foot of hills

*Logon,* marriage ceremonies, dance (at weddings)

*Lohot,,,* wet

*Lohodo:ái, lohot,, ená, kedeái,* to wet

*Loi ái, lo kedái,* draw water, strain off water

*Loi:,* penis

*Lokái ái, loká kedeái,* toss up and catch

*Lokáu,?* bend

*Loktá,* connexion, "bát," quarrel, dispute

*Lolo,* hot, warm

*Lomor,* snout (of animals)

*Lonboni:,* agent, one who carries on work for another

*Londo londo,* staring intently

*Lonká, lonkí,* man or woman weak in arms

*Lopong,* a tree

*Lorau:ái, lorau enái, kedeái,* faint, become weak, be worn out, be hungry and thirsty

*Lore,* a kind of creeper? (met.) *kathá lore en táiá* "his word was proud"

*Loroyo,* dunce, silent

*Loság ái, losá: kedeái,* snap, snarl, be angry

*Loso pondo:ái, pondoi enái, pondo kedeái,* be muddy, be dusty, roll in the dirt

*Lŏsŏt,* mud, dirty

*Lotghoti ái, kedái,* commit fornication, be quarrelsome, injure one's property

*Lŏtŏi:,* large fly

*Lotojo:ái, lotoi: enái, kedeái,* strain, sprain, hang down (as a half broken branch), bend

*Lŏtŏm ái, ená, kedeái,* deny, silence (another) overcome (habits, &c.) press down

*Lowá,* kind of fig-tree "dumbal"

*Luchá,* exacting, exorbitant

*Luchá lámot,,,* lustful, avaricious

*Lugri,* cloth, *dhotí*

*Luiyut,, luiyut,,,* aghast, astonished, very frightened, startled, coward

*Lukní,* a coarse grass

*Lulha,* wrist, hand from the wrist

*Luthu:,* successful player? the odd man at a game, a play

*Lutí,* lips

*Lutkurí,?* side of face

*Lutur,* ear

*Lutur bhugá:,* orifice of the ear

*Lutur peter,* to rub the ear (box ears)

*Lutur bíd,* erect the ear, listen

*Lutur odáu,* put hand to ear (as a person does who strives to hear)

*Lutur hupa,* part of face just below the ears

## M

*Machhá,* somewhat, like

*Máchhi,* border of a cloth

*Máchi,* chair, stool, rice-water?

*Machkáu:ái, machkáu ená, kedái, Markáu:,* } be sprained

*Madwáte,* small pox

*Mág,, eái, má: ená, kedái,* cut, attack, assault, chop

*Má: gidi,* amputate

*Má: ṭánḍí*, clear land

*Mápág*,, *áling*, *mápá: endling*, fight, mutually cut

*Má: goje ái*, *má: goi: enái*, *kedeái*, kill by sword

*Má: duṛup*, wound

*Máhákáu: á*, *máhákáu enái*, *kedeái*, stink

*Maháṇ*, day

*Maháṇder*, day before yesterday

*Máhará*, shepherd, cowherd

*Mahárog*,† plague, famine

*Máhíkal*,* a kind of bird

*Máhimá*,† glory, greatness

*Máhír*, abstinent, soft, temperate, gentle, compassionate, kind, gentleness

*Máhíro:ái*, *máhír enái*, *kedeái*, be gentle

*Mahjíd*,° mosque

*Máhkálom*, three years ago

*Máhrog*, precious, valuable, costly, dear

*Máhúr*, poison

*Máijiu*, woman, wife

*Mailá*,† filth

*Maiṇg*, said to a daughter

*Makordamá*,° affair

*Mákú*, shuttle for weaving, word used to call a sister

*Mál*,† goods, wealth, property

*Málá*,† string of beads

*Málí*, oil vessel, little lamp, gardener

*Málí bahá*, a kind of red flower

*Málkáu:ái*, *málkáu enái*, *kedái*, be wanton, glisten, lighten, shine, be ostentatious

*Málkáute*, vainly

*Málungo:ái*, *málung enái*, *kedeái*, be astonished, delighted

*Mámbṛá: mámbṛí:*, pushing, jostling, shoving, pulling

*Mán*,° a measure of 80lbs.

*Maṇ*, land received without rent for office-work done, as *manjhi*, *goret*, &c.

*Maná eái*, *kedái*,† forbid, prohibit, hinder

*Mánán ái*, *ádeái*, *kedái*,† sacrifice, vow in sickness, &c., a vow

*Manáu eái*, *enái*, *kedeái*,° love, regard, assent to, obey

*Manḍái ái*, *manḍá ená*, *kedái*, thresh

*Mándán bheḍ*, the large Sántál trumpet

*Mándár gom*, custard apple

*Mánde*, rubbish, heaps of filth, dunghill

*Mandilá táká*, the marriage rupee given to the *mánjhí* of bride's village

*Mandir*,† temple

*Mándṛáu: ái, mandṛáu enái*, fly over or about, hover, whirl

*Manḍuá*, shed erected in bride's village where the rice and *sendur* are buried at a marriage

*Mángníte*, freely, without price

*Mangṛá*,† tiles on top of roof

*Mángṛí*,* a kind of fish

*Mángṛí gocho*, moustache

*Manjái ái, ená, kedái*, scrub, clean, scour

*Mánján*, middle day meal, dinner

*Mánjhí*, the headman of a village

*Mánot*,º dignity, grandeur

*Mán̲rángre, mán̲rángte*, before (time)

*Mán̲rángreá kathá*, prophecy

*Man̲rí*, corpse

*Mán̲rom*, sheds on which the Sántáls keep their straw

*Mánsí*,? pith of a tree

*Mántár*,† a charm

*Mántár ái, kedái*,† charm

*Mámú ing*, (*m.t.*), my, thy, his uncle (mother's brother)

*Mánwá*,º human being, mankind, men

*Mánwí jánám*,º human, human race

*Mápánji*, *punchayat* of the *manjhis* of several villages

*Mápít*,,, *mápík*,º like, according to

*Máṛá:*, peacock

*Matu máṛá:*, peahen

*Máráng*, great, large, big

*Máráng engáing, engám, engát*, my, thy, his aunt (wife of father's eldest brother)

*Máráng ájing*, eldest sister

*Máráng dádá, dádám, dádát*, my, thy, his (eldest) brother

*Máráng burú*, God, demon, Satan

*Máráng dukh*, plague, pestilence

*Márán̲r bahá*,* tree with large red flowers

*Márár*, yoke

*Maráu: ái, maráu ená, kedái*,º die away, fade, be abolished, wear off (as shame, fear, &c.)

*Márchá*, worn out, uncultivated, running to weed, exhausted (as ground)

*Máre*, ancient, old

*Marí*,† plague

*Marí gutí*, small-pox

*Maṛí*, corpse, carcase, carrion (see also *maṉṛí*)

*Maṛí gaḍá*, *maṛí ṭháṇw*, *maṛí oṛá:*, grave

*Marjạd*,° honour, reverence, renown

*Maṛkáu*, sprain (see *machkáu*)

*Mársál*, light, clean, white

*Mársálo:ái*, *mársál ená*, *kedeái*, give light, be clean

*Mársálte*, brightly

*Maskúṛá*, wisdom tooth

*Másrá*,? monthly

*Másúl*,° custom, tax

*Mát*,? sow first seed of the season

*Mát*,, bamboo

*Mát*,, *ḍáng*, grove of bamboos

*Mát oṛá:*, temple, church

*Mátá mátur*,? destitute, forsaken

*Mátáleá*,° drunkard

*Mátkom*, a kind of tree, "mhowá"

*Máṭmáṭáu:ái*, *máṭáu enái*, grin, fix the teeth (sound from the noise of the teeth) eat something hard

*Máyá*,† pity, mercy

*Máyá:ái*, *máyá enái*, *ádeái*,† sympathize, feel pity, feel mercy

*Máyám*, blood

*Máyám oḍok*, bleed, have dysentery

*Máyo*, woman, coward

*Me:*, the eye

*Me: kuṭí*, eyebrows, the whole hollow formed by the eye

*Me: do*, *meṇdo*, eye disease, ophthalmia

*Me: te*, as far as eye can see

*Met*,, *áháṇ*, face

*Me: dá:*, tear

*Me: dá: joro:*, shed tears

*Met*,, *áenomo:ái*, *áenom kedái*, paint round the eyes

*Me: jápido:ái*, *jápit*,, *enái*, *kedeái*, close the eyes

*Me: jolo:*, be envious

*Me: me: gnepel*, interview

*Me: bajáu:*, cast eye upon

*Meáng*, day after to-morrow

*Mechká mechkí*, wanton, making a set at a man, shaking the head to attract attention

*Meheṇ*,? threshing-floor

*Mehuṇ*, calf

*Mehuṇ merom*, cattle (liter. calves and goats)

*Mej*,† table

*Melá, melán*, open, unenclosed, clear, wide, extended

*Men ái, kedái, met ádeái*, to say

*Men jong*, desire, wish, suppose

*Mená:*, it is

*Menáko hoṛ*, some men

*Menek*, nevertheless, but, still

*Menkhán*, but

*Meṉṛheṇt*, iron, steel

*Mente*, on account of, for, in order that

*Merá*, refuse of "mhowá" after distilling

*Meráye:*, unavailing, fruitless, useless

*Merlei:*,* a thorny tree

*Merom*, goat

*Merom me:*, a kind of tree

*Mesál eái, ená, kedái*, add, mix

*Mesál misi*, in confusion, mixed

*Met*, call, bid (see *men*)

*Metá:*, called, viz., named

*Metáme*, grant

*Metáu giḍi*,° par don

*M:i*, one, a, alike, similar, resembling

*Mimi:*, every one, each, one by one

*Mimit*,, *mimit*,, *te*, one at a time, one by one

*Mit*,, *hoṇ mit*,, every single one

*Mi: tigi, mi: te*, altogether, together

*Mi: sing mi: gnindá*, all day and night

*Mi: sámán, mi: sáuṇ*, even, level

*Mi: dháute, mi: dháu, mi: chhot*, once

*Mi: pis*,? one sided

*Mi: ṭhen*, in one place, together

*Mi: tur*, of one thickness, one layer

*Mi: jomkáu*, unanimous

*Mi: taláu*, uniformly, continually

*Mi: jok*, level, even, of one size

*Mido:, mit*,. *ocho*, to mix, mingle, resemble, unite

*Mi: monte*, sincerely, heartily

*Mi: barábarí*, resembling, alike, similar

*Mi: kathá*, faithful to one's word, agree together

*Mi: ghoṛíte*, at once, quickly

*Mi: ghoṛí khái: gi*, after a short time

*Mi: ṭung*, the slightest, the smallest [wife)

*Mi: jini*, one souled (of a

*Mi: mohndáte*, straight ahead

*Mi: lái: ren*, brother

*Mi: sir*, eunuch

*Mi: bár dháu*, occasionally

*Mi: kár goi: ákán hoṛ*, paralytic

*Mi: rogoṛte*, uniformly

*Michhạ*, in vain, falsely, contemptible worthless

*Michhạgi met*, despise

*Milág*,? join, splice

*Mil julo:ái*, *jul ená*, *kedeái*, to live on friendly terms

*Mili misi*, *mili guti*, plot, scheme

*Miloá enái*, *kedeái*, commit adultery, &c.

*Miloá ghaṭí*, fornication, adultery

*Mirju bahá*,* a kind of flowery tree

*Mirlung*, humbly

*Mirú*, a parrot

*Mís*, to plot, conspire, hold secret counsel

*Mísá:*, plot, conspiracy

*Misí ái*, *kedeái*, paint the teeth, blacken

*Misrit*,, *ái*, *ená*, *kedái*, fix (upon a plan) settle, determine, arrange

*Míṭhái*,† sweet meats

*Mithí sunum*,° a kind of oil made of *mithí* to be rubbed on body

*Mo:ái*, *mo ená*, *kedeái*, swell

*Mochá*, face, mouth

*Mochá lin*, put hand on another's mouth to prevent speaking

*Mocholká ái*, *enái*, *ocho kedeái*, make agreement, covenant

*Mochṛáu*, twist

*Mohjor*, difficult, hard

*Moh̲ndá*, appearance, direction

*Moh̲ndá:ái*, *mohndá ená*, *kedeái*, face, be turned towards

*Moh̲ndá moh̲ndí*, face to face [wards

*Mi: mohndáte*, straight to-

*Mohokubo: á*, *mohokúp*,, *ená*, *kedái*,° suspend, abolish, forbid

*Mŏhŏr meṭáu ái*, *ená*, *kedái*, destroy, die, wipe out, disappear, abolish

*Moká*, cubit

*Mo: kisni,?* toadstool

*Mokoingno:ái, mokoing enái,* complete, finish, be satisfied, have enough

*Moláu*, mortgage

*Molong*, forehead

*Molong áni:*, fortunate

*Molong tupuingno: ákin, tupuing enákin*, beat the forehead mutually

*Momoyut,,*, ashamed, sorrowful (applied to a person discovered in a fault)

*Mon*,[o] mind, heart

*Mon kháṭo:ái, enái, ocho kedeái*, be sorrowful, depressed

*Mŏndá*, the Coles

*Moṇdá: á, moṇdá enái, kedái*, spoil by keeping, become bad

*Mŏne ái, kedái*,[o] think, wish, intend, desire

*Mŏne*,[o] mind, choice, wish, desire, soul

*Mŏne rebed,,*, to love

*Mŏne achur*, repent

*Mŏne gaḍáu* or *urij,,*, apply oneself heartily, be diligent

*Mŏn gaḍáu*, pleasing

*Mŏne heju:*, come to mind, occur

*Mŏnechŏng*, what, indeed

*Moṉj, moṉják,,*, good, good-looking, good to talk, beautiful, pretty

*Moṉreko turuiko*, one of the Sántál gods (*lit.*, the fives and sixes)

*Morá*, thin, lean, feeble, weak, powerless

*Moṛái*, increase in size (as growing rice)

*Morá muháṉr*, the south, the point to which the Sántáls turn when burying their dead

*Moron*,[o] death

*Mosodo: á, mosot,, ená, kedái*, fade away (as trees, &c.), wither

*Mosolá*,[o] spices

*Moste*, see "muste"

*Moṭá*,† fat, bass voice

*Moṭá anjom*, hear with difficulty

*Moṭá ruaṛo:*, become strong again, fat after sickness

*Moṭge*, by force, tyrannically, oppressively

*Moṭ sáp*, compel to do work

*Moṭrá*,[o] bundle

*Moṭrá juṭrái ái, moṭrá juṭrá enú kedái,* goods and chattels, parcels and pack

*Moṭyám,* seize, grasp, take

*Muchạt,* top, end, the back part

*Muchạtre,* finally

*Muchhí huṛú,* black rice

*Muchí,*° drum makers (a caste)

*Muchu,* open basket (for fishing)

*Muchur muchur jom,* to munch, eat, make noise in eating

*Mudá,?* stolen goods

*Muḍu lái:* small entrails

*Mug,** a kind of pulse

*Muhin, muhim,* risk, danger, affliction

*Muiṇ* ant

*Muiṇ leká,* crowded

*Mukhạrat,*° face to face

*Mukhiyá,*† chief, principal person

*Muktáu:,* be full

*Muktí,*† pearl

*Mukulte,?* perform ceremonies after childbirth

*Mul ái, ená, kedái,*† appraise, value, appoint, fix, settle, give pattern

*Mule habádo: á, habát„ kedái,* destroy

*Mulíno:ái, mulín enái, kedeái,*° be sorrowful, sad

*Mul, mur,*† pattern, original. primary

*Mului: mului:,* a smile

*Muṇ,*° nose

*Muṇ bhugạ:,* nostrils

*Muṇd,* among

*Mundáu: á, mundáu enái, kedeái,* close up (hole, &c.), close in, join

*Muṇdhát„,* logs, blocks of wood

*Muṇdoi,*° plaintiff

*Munḍrá,*° shaved head

*Munḍu,* jungle

*Munís,* servant

*Múṉrdám? muṇdám, mudám,* ring

*Murái,* crib, manger, granary, "tek"

*Murchháu: á, murchháu ená, kedái,*° rust, corrode, square the end of a log, smooth with adze, &c.

*Murgá,* a kind of tree, "piasal"

*Murhui: jom,* leprosy

*Murhui: jomi:,* leper

*Murhut„*° image, idol

*Muru:,* a kind of tree

*Murúbe,*° aged man, elder

*Muruko:ái, muruk enái, ocho*

*kedeái*, be attentive, apply diligently, lean against, press against

*Muskíl*,° arduous, difficult

*Mussá*, silent

*Muste em*, lend, have for nothing, receive for nothing

*Muṭo:ái, muṭ kedái*, draw a sword, catch hold as one would of a sword, grasp

*Mutak*, staff, thick stick

*Muthá*, a low kind of grass

*Muṭhạn*, image, appearance

*Muthní*, summit, top, peak

*Mutul kátup* middle finger

*Mutul khunṭí*, longest and middle pillars of a house

N

*Nabí*,† prophet

*Náchu*, a basket placed to catch fish

*Nádo:*,? to practise austerities

*Nafá*,† advantage

*Nagráhá, nangráhá*,° city

*Nahá:*, now

*Nahá: jug*, the present time

*Náhak*,° worthless, in vain

*Nahaká:*,° vanity

*Nahel*, plough

*Nahel gáṛá* or *gaḍá*, furrow

*Naí*, the Damoda River into which the Sántáls throw their dead

*Náib*,† deputy

*Náikki*, Sántál priest

*Náiṉnu*, butter

*Nakhá*, side

*Náki:*, a comb

*Nákijo:ái, náki: kedeái*, comb

*Naksá*,° drawing, picture

*Nálá*,† channel, ditch, drain

*Nálhá*, wages, food for work

*Nálhá jong*, make a livelihood

*Nális ái, ená, ádeái*,° complain, have a lawsuit

*Námdák*,° well-known, notorious, celebrated, renowned

*Nána hunạr*,° different kinds

*Nánḍá, náṉrá*, some rice left in the field for the poor

*Nangá*,° devotee

*Nángŏs ái, kedái*, pretend

*Nangráhá*,° city, bazaar (see also *nagráhá*)

*Nánhá*, thin, fine, nice, slight, slender (as a stick, &c.)

*Nanjom*, witch

*Nanrí*, a creeper (plant)

*Nápáio:*, be established, be settled, be good, be clean

*Nápái okoi:*, very good

*Napṛá:*, great, large

*Narí*,† pulse

*Náṛi chaaṛá*,* a kind of vegetable

*Naṛ joṛo: ákin, jor enákin, het kinái*, marry

*Nárkoṛ*, cocoa nut

*Narṛi*, throat

*Náse*, false, light, foolish, vain, a little

*Náse seturá*, thoughtless, vain, giddy

*Nátíkár, koṛáring erá*, granddaughter

*Nátí koṛáring*, grandson

*Naṭwá*, to reel silk

*Náwán*, fresh, new, recent

*Náuṇ*, barber

*Nawágṇi*, to offer in sacrifice, present firstfruits

*Ne*, take (imperative); *neho*, to a man; *neyáṇ*, to a child

*Ne betár*, now, these times

*Nee*, this indeed

*Ne párom*, this side

*Ne nahá:*, now, immediately

*Neáo*,° to decide, determine, settle

*Nehạdo:ái, nehạt" enái, hedeái*, be little, small, despised

*Nehoro:ái, nehor enái, hedeái*, be zealous, be earnest, beseech, entreat, ask earnestly, pray, importune

*Nehot eái, ená, hedeái*, press down, disobey (a command), deny, despise, contemn

*Neṇḍá*, covenant, agreement, arrangement, stipulated

*Nenkán*, thus

*Neotá eái, hedeái*,† invite, give a feast.

*Nes*, this year

*Níá*, this (neut.)

*Nichhurá*, spotless, quite clean

*Níchind*, unawares, ignorant

*Níchŏl*, desolate, lonely, solitary

*Nídandí*, safe, secure, unconcerned

*Nidharúá*, rich, free from debt

*Níhạt eái, ená, hedeái*, think small of, despise, scorn [see also *nehạdo:*]

*Nihạtge*, very little

*Nijáu:ái, nijáu enái, hedái*, be recovering from drunkenness, get well by medicine

*Nijhúm*, lonely, solitary, calm, still

*Níjor*,° weak, weakness

*Níjrúá*, hale, well

*Nikhaṛ ái, enái, kedeái,* get perfectly well, to recover entirely

*Ním,* a kind of tree, "ním"

*Nimbrot eái, enái, kedeái,* soften, appease, be reconciled

*Níṇa:, nínáng, niṇa: báṛe,* } so
,, *níṇa: ge* }
many, so, thus much or many

*Níndáu,*° to slander

*Níṇdhán,* gentle, low, small

*Niṇghá,* axletree

*Niphuṭ,* hale, well, pure, sinless, unmixed, unbroken, unarmed, one of a pair when the mate has died, *e.g.* one bullock

*Nirá,*† pure, unmixed

*Nirá mone,* pure-minded, singleminded

*Nirbáh,*† daily fare

*Nirbudh,*° ignorant, stupid

*Nirghin,* disfigured through sorrow, heart struck

*Niron,* warmth, sunshine

*Niron din,* summer

*Nistár,*† salvation, deliverance

*Nisún,*° empty, void, desolate, deserted

*Nit, níto, níto do, nítgi, nít báṛe,* now

*Nít hábí:,* until now

*Nit sahí,?* exact, true

*Niurá,?* anklet

*Noláu: á, noláu ená, kedeái,* prepare, investigate, examine

*Nŏṇḍe,* here, in this place

*Nŏṇḍená,* of, or belonging to, this place

*Nŏnká, nŏnkán,* so, thus

*Nonkáte,* in this manner

*Nonkái ái, nonká ená, kedái,* do so

*Nonkán ái,* be so

*No párom,* this side

*Nŏsíb,*° fate, fortune

*Nosíb ánái,* fortunate

*Nosṭo eái, enái, kedeái,* destroy, annihilate

*Nŏte,* here, hither

*Noteá,* a call to any one

*Notená,* the (things) of this side

*Núá, núi,* this, it, this person

*Nuá hábi:,* until now

*Nuáte,* therefore, whereupon, on this, for this reason

*Nuṇa, nun,* so much, so many

*Nuṇang,* thus much

*Nuṇa habi:* insomuch, so that

*Nun máráng,* thus big

*Nunu áiái ádeái,* suckle, nurse

*Nyút,* dark, darkness

*Nyúto: á, nyút enái, kedeái,* become dark, be benighted

## O

*O:*, smoke

*O: á, o: ená, hedeái,* to smoke

*O: goje:*, to suffocate by smoke

*Oár,* deliverance, salvation

*Oáris,* helper, saviour

*Oáro:ái, oár ená, kedeái,* extricate, deliver, rescue

*Ochŏg,, o:ái, ocho: ená, kedeái,* clear the way, remove, take away, transfer to another place

*Ochut,,*, hump of bull, fireplace

*Odá,* wetted

*Odám,* otter

*Oḍáu ái, ená, kedeái,* spread out

*Oḍo: á, oḍ ená, kedeái,* shelter, protect, defend

*Oḍoko:ái, oḍok ená, kedeái,* come or go or bring out, extract, expel

*Oḍung,* come out

*Ofsor,*° opportunity, leisure, means [See also *afsor*]

*Ogher,*? be insensible

*Oho,* What a pity!

*Ohŏráu: á, ohoráu ená, kedái,* assuage, decrease, become gradually silent, lessen, abate, diminish

*Ojhá,* doctor, physician, teacher of charms

*Ojo,* boil, abscess

*Ojogo:ái, ojo: ená, kedeái,* grease, rub on oil, &c.

*Oká,* what

*Oká leká,* in what way, how

*Oká se:,* where, whither, in what direction or side

*Oká khon,* whence

*Oká hilo:, oká ghoṛi,* when, what time

*Oká ṭhenre,* in what place, in the place which

*Oká te,* whither

*Okáṭá te,* in what, wherever

*Oká re,* where, anywhere

*Okáre hoṇ báng,* nowhere

*Oká báte,* how quickly!

*Oká tehoṇ,* by any means

*Okáte hoṇ báng,* by no means

*Oká do,* occasionally

*Oká bhaḍgte,* uncertainly, with difficulty, who knows how

*Oko:ái, okoi enú, kedeái*, hide, conceal (also *okun* in present and future tenses)

*Okore*, privately, secretly

*Okun ṭhen*, a hiding-place

*Okoe*, who

*Okoi:*, many (in comp.); as *aḍí okoí:*

*Oktá mángál*, a reproach, bye-word

*Oktáu áiái, ádeái*, despise, slander, spread reports, tell tales

*Okte machhá*, season, the proper season

*Okte okte*,° at times, at proper seasons

*Ol:* writing

*Olo: á, ol kedái*, to write, draw (pictures), spoil, become bad, fade, dry, wither (as leaves), be musty

*Olá:*, written paper

*Ol bándhi*,? arrest

*O:oli:*, a writer, an author

*Oláng-mocháng*, greedy, pick-pocket, thievish (particularly used of cattle)

*Oloingno:ái, oloing enái, kedeái*, be troubled, cast down, frightened, sad, sorrowful

*Olŏm jhŏlŏm*, finery, ornaments

*Ombágo:ái, ombá: enái, kedeái*, kneel

*Omono: á, omon ená, kedái*, germinate, spring forth (as seeds), shoot out, be born

*Oná*, that (thing)

*Oná leká, onkáge*, like that, in that manner, &c.

*Onágese, onechŏng*, that indeed

*Oná hoṇ*, that even, that also

*Oná te, oná mente* / *Oná teráng* } therefore, for that cause, whereupon, at this

*Oná mahánḍer*, three days ago

*Onḍe*, there, that place

*Onḍgá*, those who sacrifice human beings, "Thugs"

*Ong ái, kedái*, blow

*Ongsŏng*, friendship, peace, friend

*On jolo:*,° to eat and drink, to take refreshment

*Onmán ái, kedái*, investigate, perceive, discover

*On párom*, that side

*Onŏl gŏnŏl*, checked, checquered

*Onte*, thither

*Onte nŏte*, hither and thither

*Onte note: áko, note enáko, ketkoai*, scatter

*Ontor*,° heart

*Opát*,,, young tree (very small)

*Opŏr áling, ená*, pull in different directions

*Opor jopor chalá:*, to follow close upon, be hard upon

*Oṛá:*, house, dwelling

*Oṛág ái, oṛá: enái, kedái*, make a house, dwell, inhabit

*Oṛá: grosti ko*, members of a family

*Orá parí*, turn and turn about

*Ordá:*, snare birds

*Oṛe*, quail

*Oṛejo:ái, oṛe: enái, kedái*, burst, rend, tear, tear in pieces

*Oṛe: háting*, split into half

*Oṛe:*, rent, fissure, gap

*Oṛheṇo:ái, oṛheṇ enái, kedeái*, praise, recount deeds, celebrate fame

*Oṛlo*, dull, silly, stupid, ignorant, obtuse, fool

*Oṛmŏi:*, bug

*Oro:ái, or ená, kedeái*, draw, pull, drag with the hands

*Or asíd*, to tie in a slip knot

*Oroch*,? want of appetite

*Oroj*,° petition, request

*Orojo:ái, oroj kedái*, beseech, apply, make request

*Orong ái, kedái*, play, blow an instrument

*O:rongi:*, musician

*Orop koṭop*,* a wild esculent root

*Ortáb ái, ortáp*,, *ená, kedeái*, draw through

*Orwál*,† awning, screen, veil for women, a kind of bird

*Osár*, wide, extended, broad

*Osogo:ái, oso: enái, kedeái*, worn out, thin (from sickness)

*Oso: koti*, become thin

*Osoráu*, to begin, prepare

*Ot*,, *kisni, ot*,,, toadstool, mushroom

*Ot*,, *gopá:* } different
*Ot*,, *dá: mánde* } kinds of mushrooms

*Ot*, world, earth

*Ot ot te*, on foot, by land

*Ot hiláu:*, earthquake

*Oṭágo: á, oṭá: ena, kedái*, open (a book), uncover

*Oṭángo:ái, oṭáng ená, kedeái,* winnow by letting the grains fall about, fly, throw up in air, dissipate, squander

*Otet,*[m] valley

*Otong eái, kedeái,* follow, chase

*Otong táyom,* one after another, in turn, before and after, order, caste, successful

*Otoṛo: á, otoṛ ená, kedeái,* raze, break down (house, fence, &c.)

*Oyo:ái, oyoi enái, oyo kedeái,* wrap one's self up, clothe one's self

*O yo: á:, oyoná:,* garments, vestments

*Oyŏng ái, kedeái,* peep, look down upon, stoop to look

*Oyug ái, oyu: enái, kedeái,* strike with sword, be born

P

*Päāg dŏn,* sword dance

*Pách,*? bleed, let blood

*Pacháu: á, pacháu ená, kedái,*[o] digest food

*Pachhái ái, pachhá kedái,* lay hold of a fault, reckon, consider, find out

*Pachhim,*† west

*Páchil,*[o] load a cart too heavily behind, walk backwards

*Pachilá,* hinder part of a cart

*Pachilạ enái, pạch kedeái,* walk backwards

*Pachnáu:ái, pachnáu enái, kedeái,* recognise

*Pachrí,* fence, enclosure, hedge

*Pachrí achur,* fortify, enclose a village by earth, &c.

*Paḍhua,*? sluggard

*Páerá ái, kedái,* swim

*Páerá baṛái,* wander about be a vagabond

*Págur ái, kedái,* chew the cud

*Pahá poho,* dawn

*Páhíl,*[o] first

*Páhíláunṭá,* firstborn

*Páhílre,* first, before, in advance, already, anciently

*Pakṭá,* piece, strip, division

*Páhuṛ,* sacrifice

*Paihạ,* follower, pupil, disciple

*Páik,*? messenger

*Páilá,* a measure about one quart

*Páinchí,* long pieces of cloth (as *dhotis, chaddars,* &c.)

*Páingán,* anklet with bells (put on at dances, &c.)

*Páisá*,† pence, coppers, money

*Pájhár*, kite

*Páji*,° scoundrel

*Pakáre*,* a kind of tree

*Pakhá*, shelf, niche

*Páktá*,?° ripe, cooked, grown to maturity, full grown

*Pál*, ploughshare

*Pálá*,° power, authority, control, state

*Pálák*, bed, cot

*Pálák párkom*, a large kind of bed

*Páláng*, saddle of a horse or ox

*Páláng ái, kedái*, spread out,? put on a saddle

*Palá: pologo: á, polo: enái*, to be dim (as the eye)

*Pálāṭo:ái, páláṭ enái, kedeái*, change clothes

*Pálo: á, páloi ená, pálo kedái*, grow white (as drying leaves)

*Pán*,† betel "pán"

*Pán rán*, medicine

*Pánáhi*, shoes, slippers

*Pánchá em*, lend, advance money for a short time

*Panchí*, small and light *chaddar*

*Pánde*, groin

*Pánḍit*,† learned

*Pándolo:ái, pándol ená, kedeái*, miss a chance, beat, surpass, excel, conquer, defeat, push away, overcome, press down

*Pándráhi*, filthy, disgusting, dirty, untidy, uncleanly

*Panḍu: á, panḍui ená, panḍu kedai*, become grey or hoary, wither, dry as leaves

*Panḍu úp*, white hair

*Pánjá*, footprint

*Pánjái eái, pánjá ená, kedeái*, trace, pursue, track, follow, search, leave footmarks

*Panjá tiog*,,, overtake

*Panjár*, rib

*Panjrí*, frame of cart, the pieces of wood put crossways in a native *gáṛí*

*Pánk*, bottom of river

*Pánmuhiri*,* spices, "soṇp"

*Pánte: ále, pánte enále, ket koái*, sit or walk in a row

*Pánṭilo:ái, pánṭil enái, kedái*, bound off, spring up, jump up

*Panwár gocho*, whiskers

*Páp*,† sin

*Pápi*, sinful

*Páṛá*,? cockfighting-place

*Pāṛá:*, rent, crack (in wood ground, &c)

*Paṛá: chhirchatur*, split into pieces

*Paṛágo: á, paṛá: ená, kedái*, split, rend, divide

*Párágáṛe*, overhear,? spy,? discover secretly, wander about saunteringly

*Parámáp*,? bespeak

*Parámes*,?[o] to advise, consult

*Parámánik*, prime minister of the *mánjhi*, second man in the village

*Páṛáu: á, páṛáu ená*,[o] be, fall, obtain

*Paráunchá*, stands on which the Sántáls keep their straw

*Párcháu: á, parcháu ená, kedái*, be plentiful (as flowers) spread, increase

*Párgáná*, chief Sántál officer, with from twenty to sixty villages under him

*Parháu ái, kedeái*, read, study

*Pári-párite*, take by, or in, turns

*Pári ruạ*, intermittent fever

*Pariạ*, time, generation

*Páris*, generation, tribe, caste, family

*Párkom*, bed, cot

*Paṛlak*, stripe on the borders of a cloth

*Párlek*, almost, perhaps, possibly

*Párom*, over, beyond

*Páromo:ái, párom ená, kedeái*, cross over, convey over [through

*Párom chalá:*, pass by, or

*Pársí, phársi*, language

*Párwá*, dove

*Pásáro: á, pásár ená, kedái*, fly open, spread out

*Páse, parlek*, if, lest

*Pasí:*, net for birds

*Pasí:ái, pasí enái, kedeái*, catch or be caught, entrap, catch in talk, find out

*Pásiro: á, pásir ená, kedái*, scatter, fly about, rebound, fly off as chips

*Páskái ái, páská kedái*, scrape with the foot

*Paskáu*, escape, slip away (see *phaskáu*)

*Pásnáu:á, pásnáu ená, kedái*, spread, be or make known, circulate, publish, scatter

*Pásuṛo:ái, pásuṛ enái, kedeái*, slip away, let slip, work in vain

*Pátá*, board, slate

*Páṭáhárháng*,* a spotted poisonous snake

*Pátái ái, pátá enái, kedái,* swing on hooks (as devotees)

*Pátáṛá:,* split wood

*Patár patár,* to gnaw

*Pátáṛ potoṛ,* bush, bushes, shrubs

*Páṭár poṭor,* hairless, featherless (used of birds, animals), destitute of grass

*Páṭáu ái, kedái,* level floor by pounding, smear floor, water flowers

*Páṭchelá,* scholar, one who lives with a *guṛú*

*Páṭgánḍo:ái, gánḍoi enái, gánḍo kedeái,* sit on ground with legs crossed

*Páṭh,*† lesson, reading task

*Páṭhá, páṭhí,*† kid (male and female), lamb,? pig?

*Páṭhe:ái, páṭhe enái, kedeái,* bind clothes tight, gird the loins

*Pathrí,* the art of throwing charms known to "ojhas" by which the person thrown at dies, ejecting spittle at a person

*Páṭí ái, ená, kedeái,* bore, make a hole, prick

*Paṭiá,* mat (made of palm leaves)

*Patiáu:ái, patiáu enái, kedái,* believe, credit, have faith, feel confidence

*Páṭiháro:ái, paṭihár enái, kedeái,* draw blood from one's body as the Sántál "gurus" do

*Páṭi jilád eái, jilát,, ená, kedeái,* nail up, fix, fasten

*Páṭká,* tough

*Patṛá,* flat plate of leaves

*Páṭsir,?* heel ropes

*Paṭṭá,* old, tough (as chicken), rotten (as meal, &c.), lease

*Páṭṭá sákám,*° lease

*Páṭub ái, páṭup,, enái, kedeái,* root out, tear up by roots, lever up

*Páṭwet,,,* deceitful, crafty

*Paurá,* a liquor made by Sánṭáls

*Paurá chuạ,* grog shop

*Páyá,* lake, pool

*Páyár idí,* sway in one direction by wind

*Peádá,*° messenger, soldier, policeman

*Peáj,*° onion

*Peláu: á, peláu enái, kedeái,* force a passage

*Peṇcho:ái, peṇch enái, kedeái,* overcome, press down, narrow, make small

*Penḍko, peṇrko:, peṇrolko:,* unripe

*Pepṇret*, trumpet, flute
*Peṛá*, friend, relative
*Peṛái eái, peṛá ená, kedeái*, entertain friends, make friends
*Peṛá pahánṛá*, friends and relatives
*Pere: á:*, fulness, filled
*Perej„o: á, pere: ená, kedeái*, be filled, be full
*Peṛsango: á, peṛsang ená, kedeái*, glance off
*Pese:*, triangular
*Peská*, testicle
*Peṭ dándiá*, glutton
*Peṭe: lipí*, blasted grain
*Peṭe peṭe*, crowded, jammed together
*Peṭerbáre*,* a kind of tree
*Peṭero: á, peṭer ená, kedái*, twist
*Phaḍaḍ*, army, crowd [open
*Phádá*, unenclosed, exposed,
*Phádá phudu*, fluttering
*Pháiláo*,° renowned, firmament, expanse
*Phákuṇrá*,? ear of corn
*Phándái ái, phándá kedeái*, kick as a horse
*Phánk*, vain, empty, dear
*Pháph uḍáute*, sneeringly, mockingly, ridiculingly, laughingly
*Phárákho: á, phárak ená, kedeái*, separate one's self
*Phaṛchhá*, clear (as the sky), evident, open
*Pháṛí*, a quarter of meat, shoulder
*Phariạ:ái, phariạ enái, kedeái*, recover from sickness, cure, become well [ness
*Phariạmone*, pureminded-
*Pharkáu:ái, pharkáu enái, kedeái*, fly away
*Phársí*, language, tongue (also *páṛsi*) [noose
*Phásí*, deceit, difficulty, snare,
*Phásí:ái, phásí enái, kedeái*, hang, kill
*Phásíḍáng*, gallows
*Phasiạṛá ái, enái, kedái*, deceive, defraud, inveigle
*Phasiạṛá*, deceiver
*Phaskáu: á, phaskáu enái, kedeái*,? escape, let go, slip, away
*Phás phus*, conspiracy, plot
*Phásuṛo: á, phásuṛ ená, kedeái*, fruitless, in vain, slip away
*Pháṭár pháṭáro: á, pháṭár ená, kedái*, devour, gnaw, make a noise in eating
*Pháṭoko:ái, pháṭok enái, kedeái*,° shut up, confine
*Pháṭok*,° a prison

*Phautí*, useless, rejected, masterless, ownerless, neglected, lazy, idle, empty (house,&c.)

*Pheder phedero:ái, pheder enái*, complain, mutter, chatter in anger

*Phedo: á, phe: ená, kedeái*, fly back and hit (as boughs)

*Phen*, parable

*Phen roṛ*, speak in parables

*Phente*, enigmatically

*Phenchoṛo: á, phenchoṛ ená, kedái*, glance off, rebound

*Phenkáu:ái, phenkáu enái, kedeái*, conceal from justice, stray, wander, drive away, run away

*Phenro:ái, phenr enái, kedeái*,° foam, froth

*Pheṭánr*, heifer

*Phepṛá:ái, phepṛái enái*, act the hypocrite, simulate ignorance, stumble

*Pheṛ, pheḍ*, near, by side of, bottom, below

*Pheṛ khon*, from the beginning or bottom

*Pheṛte*, low, near the ground

*Pheṛ re*, in the neighbourhood

*Pher enderái*, three days after tomorrow

*Pher sátom*,? three years hence

*Pher baipár*,° trade of a money-lender, traffic

*Pher ke pher*, again, back again

*Pheṛpáng*,? sink in the mud, stick in the mud

*Pher phár*, changes

*Phikir ái, kedái*,° contrive, be cunning, deceive

*Phink leka*, very white

*Phínphíniyá*, very fine and white clothes

*Phiráu: á, phiráu enái, kedeái*,° restore, give back, alter, change, change colour

*Phirí*, shield

*Phiṛipháng*, cloudless

*Phirkodo:ái, phirkot„ enái, kedeái*, sullen, silent (of a woman)

*Phirphiri*,? jewel

*Phirphiro:ái, phir enái, kedeái*, be angry (of a woman) kick quickly (as a cow)

*Phiṭkirí*,† alum

*Phográ*, toothless

*Phŏká: á, phokái ená, phoká kedeái*, blister, fester

*Phŏká*, blister from burning

*Phoko phoko*, be very fat

*Phokphoko:ái, phokoi enái, phoko kedái*, foam

*Phoktiá*, wit, ridicule

*Phŏphundá*, musty, stale, dusty, dirty

*Phormásái ái, phormás kedái,*° bespeak

*Phoṛo: á, phoṛ ená, kedái,* burst forth (as water)

*Phoro:?* °crumble

*Phorphundí*, hypocrisy, fraud, artful, deceitful

*Phoṭá: á, phoṭá ená, kedeái,* be skinned (by a burn, blister, &c.), peel

*Phudphudáu:ái, phudáu enái, kedeái,* clap wings

*Phuktí, phŏktiá,* fun, mirth, quaintness

*Phukut,, phukut,,,* dying, at the last gasp, rumbling in stomach

*Phuláu:ái, phuláu enái, kedeái,* be proud, distend

*Phulí*, strong liquor before water is added

*Phúlí*, mote, eyeball

*Phúlpatáu*, friendship, communion, concord; give gifts, mutually in token of friendship

*Phundi,?* make false excuses (see *phorphundi*)

*Phuphuáu ái, ádeái,* breathe hard, snort

*Phuṛog ái, phuṛo: kedái,* make cups of leaves

*Phuṛog,,,* cup of leaves

*Phusláu eái, kedeái,*° flatter, inveigle

*Phusphus, phusphusrŏṛ*, whisper

*Phuṭ*, melon; split, a sudden snap (of rope, &c.)

*Phuṭáu: á, phuṭáu ená, kedái,* break forth, be revealed (as secrets)

*Pichhaurí*, sheet, the large cloth worn in winter by men, but single

*Piko poko:ái, pokoi enái, poko kedeái,* be fat-cleeked, corpulent

*Píla*, spleen

*Pilchu háṉrám*, the first man

*Pilchu buḍḍhí*, the first woman

*Pindá*, verandah

*Pínḍḍ*, altar

*Pinká,?* cigar

*Pípá,*† cask

*Pipiriáng*, butterfly

*Pipní*, eyeball, apple of eye

*Píṛhí*, generation

*Piri,?* snake basket

*Piṛiáng piṛiáng ái, kedái,* cry as a bird

*Piṛiá piṛiá*, just dying, at the last gasp

*Piring,?* misconduct

*Piri: pirijo: á, piri: enái, kedái,* ooze out, sun just appearing

*Piríto: áling, pirít enái, kedeái,*[o] long for, love, feel great affection for

*Pisír,* to open, distend, *pasír*

*Piskij,* part the grass in search of something

*Pít,*† gall; a sickness (like smallpox or itch)

*Pítal,*† brass

*Piṭhạ,* bread, loaf

*Piṭí:,* skein of hemp, a kind of girdle worn at sword dance

*Piṭíjo:ái, piṭi: enái, kedái,* coil up (as snake), be matted (as hair, &c.), wind up

*Piṭuk,*[o] glutton

*Piyáng páyáng,* dawn, just beginning to get light

*Pochá,** a kind of fish

*Pochrá,* cowardly

*Podíná,*† mint

*Podná,* string worn round the arm

*Poḍo,* fig tree

*Podo:ái, pod enái, kedeái,* remove, have two places of residence, change villages

*Pohá,* plant

*Pohá: á, pohá ená,* bud (as a tree)

*Poho,* locust

*Poi,* result of an evil act, consequences, punishment

*Pokpoko:ái, pokoi enái, poko kedái,* puff out the cheeks, be fat (see also *phoko phoko*)

*Pŏkrŏk,?* ugly

*Pokrot,,,* corpulent, flabby, fat-cheeked

*Polo: polo:,* hardly visible, indistinct

*Ponḍá:ái, ponḍ kedái,* whiten

*Ponḍ,* white, clean

*Pondá,* rotten wood, wood hard on one side and soft on the other

*Pon,* four

*Ponjángáwán,* quadruped

*Ponhonḍ,* square, four-cornered, all round

*Poṛ,* low scrubby jungle

*Poráiní,* a white lily

*Porho,* result, fruit, confidence

*Pormondá,* tyranny, oppression

*Pŏrŏb,* festival, feast

*Pŏrŏbo:ái, porob enái, kedái,* to keep a festival

*Poroi poroi dá:,* showers

*Poságo: á, posá: ená, kedái,* fly open, break in pieces, snap break

*Poská*, soft, week (generally of wood or cotton)

*Posṛá eái, kedeái*, despise, scorn

*Pŏstá*, doe

*Poṭá*, stomach

*Poṭágo: á, poṭá: ená, kedeái*, peel bark from trees, peel off (the skin)

*Potám*, dove

*Pŏtásír*, large vein

*Poṭáu ái, ená, kedái*, smear, plaister with mud (see *paṭáu*)

*Poṭiyá tárup*, tiger

*Poṭojo: á, poṭoi: ená*, be sprained, out of joint

*Poṭomo: á, poṭom enái, kedeái*, wrap up

*Poṭom mid*,,, wrap up together, enclose

*Poṭoro: á, poṭor ená, kedeái*, cleanse, dress (a fowl, &c.), pluck feathers, dig up grass, steal clothes

*Poṭrá*, corpulent, large stomach (as in spleen)

*Powá*, a weight about one pound

*Púchháu eái, kedeái*,° ask into a house, invite, entertain, treat kindly

*Puḍi*,* a kind of fish

*Puhí*,? float of fishing-line

*Pui pui ái, enái, kedeái*, surfeit

*Puj*,? matter from a sore

*Pujá aghá*,° idolator

*Pukrí*,° tank

*Pul*,† bridge

*Pungí*, tobacco-pipe made of leaves

*Pupulhet*,,, hazy, pale moonlight

*Púrab*,† east

*Purái*,* a kind of vegetable or fruit, "paiság"

*Puráu: á, puráu ená, kedeái*,° fulfil, accomplish, full price, &c.

*Purhút bábṛen*, Brahmins

*Púrí*, world

*Purkhạ*,° old men, elders

*Puruchhun*, excellence, merit

*Púrún*,° complete, faultless, perfect, full

*Pusí*, cat

*Pusindo: ái, pusind kedái*,° please, choose, like, select

*Pusrí*, prickly heat

*Pustak, puthí*,† book

*Pusṭáu ái, kedái*, pronounce clearly, articulate

*Puṭhujo: ái, puṭhui: enái, kedái*, sprain, remove entrails, gut

*Puṭi: ái, puṭi enái, kedeái*, bloat, not to digest food

*Putlạ*, idol,? a piece of a cart

## R

*Rábáng*, cold
 *Rábáng din*, winter
*Rábor ái, enái, kedeái*, scratch
*Rách*, part of weaver's apparatus
*Ráchá ái, kedeái*, go to stool
 *Ráchá*, compound, garden
 *Ráchá te*, outside (*i.e.*, the house)
*Ráchágo: á, ráchá: enái, kedeái*, break off, pluck off, pull out, pick off
*Ráddahá*, evil person, vile person
*Rádrádáu*, drag along ground, haul along ground (make the sound of "rad, rad"), crackle
*Ráekákánrbá*, chameleon
*Rág ái, rá: kedeái*, cry, whine, wail for dead, scream
 *Rárá: i:*, crier
 *Rá: jarwá*, call together
*Rágumchá:*, with coarse dishevelled hair; a kind of root
*Ráhám*, salted, over-seasoned
*Rahan, rohon*, employment, trade, occupation, customary work
*Raháu: á, raháu ená, kedái*, sleep, as hand or foot
*Raher*, a kind of pea, "rahar"
*Ráhí*, steady,? peaceful,? mild,? *palki*
*Rái*,[O] a caste of this name
*Rai*,[O] mustard
*Ráibári:*, angel,? arranger of marriages
*Rái duhái*,[O] supplication
*Ráj*,† zemindar, king, landlord, magistrate
 *Rájo:ái, ráj enái, kedeái*,[O] be a king, reign
 *Ráj rapáj*, sovereign, king, magistrates
 *Ráj disom*,[O] country
 *Ráj dháni*, palace
*Ráji:ái, ráji enái, kedeái*,[O] be pleased, consent, be willing
*Rájá muni*, a kind of bird
*Ráján bháján*, splendour, hospitable, magnificent (giving many *gharas* of grog at a wedding)
*Rákábo:ái, rákáp" enái, kedeái*, raise
*Rakhni*,? prohibition, embargo
*Rámá*, nails, claws
*Rámpá ái, rámpái ená, rámpá kedeái*, surround with thorns
*Rán, rándá:*, medicine
 *Rán, rán taká*, bribe
*Randkap*,* a kind of fish

*Ránákháp*, notches to ascend by, kind of steps

*Ránbŏrá*,? "dál," a kind of pea, "biri"

*Randí*,† widow

*Rángá chŏngá*, knotted, gnarled, rough (as trees), thorny

*Rangáini*, a wide-spreading weed like a thistle

*Rangáu:ái, rangáu enái, kedeái*, be indignant

*Ráni*,† a queen

*Ránre*,? relent

*Rának*,† rays of sun, light

*Ránu*, drug put into liquor to make it intoxicating, leaven

*Rápáboṛ áling, enáling*, tear with nails, mutually scratch (see *ráboṛ*)

*Rápáchá: áling*, fight, seize by hair mutually (see *rácháġ*)

*Rápág eái, rápá: enái, kedeái*, burn the dead, cook, roast

*Ráprápá: ái, ráprápá enái, kedeái*, have disorderly hair, fence with thorns, sprawl on ground

*Rápudo: á, ráput„ enái, kedeái*, break, crack, crumble, pierce

*Raṛ ái, kedái*, sing sweetly, sound sweet

*Ráṛái ái, ráṛá ená, kedeái*, let go, loosen, open, free, release, unbind, untie

*Ráṛo: á, ráṛ akáná*, tumble, foam (as a river through rocks)

*Raṣ*, produce of the earth

*Rásá*,[o] juice, honey

*Ráse*, soup, juice of meat

*Rásiá áling, enáling, kedáling*, share together, have partneship

*Rásiáte*, together

*Rásít*,[o] receipt

*Raskạ:ái, raskạ enái, kedái*, desire

*Raskạ*, delight, desire, wish

*Rassi áto, rassi bŏstí*, large village, town, city

*Rásun*,[o] garlic.

*Rátá kuṛí*, girl past the age of marriage

*Rátáng*, frost, snow

*Ráth*,[o] car, rays of sun

*Ráth gaḍí*, chariot

*Rau*,? fly

*Ráuráu:ái, ráuráu kedeái*, make a noise, or row, crackle (as fire), scold

*Ráwál*, easy, light

*Re*, in, among, between, against

*táláre*, in the midst, among, between

*Reáṛ*, cold, cool

*Reáṛo:ái, reáṛ enái, ke dingná*, become cold, or numb

*Rebedo: á, rebet„ kedái*, crowd in, hide, tuck up, push in, squeeze in

*Reben*, consent

*Rebeno:ái, reben enái, kedeái*, agree, be willing, desire, like, consent, wish

*Rechŏng*, perhaps (in comp.)

*Rehḍá*, kind of earth of which cows are fond

*Rehet„*, root, foundation

*Rehedo: á, rehet„ ená, kedái*, take root

*Rej ái, re: kedái*, take by force, ravish, rob, seize, steal

*Rere: á:*, spoil, theft, stolen property

*Rejimeng*, chatterer, talkative (of women)

*Relo: á, rel ená, kedái*, winnow in a fan [hold

*Remo: á, rem ená, kedeái*, take

*Reme:*, part of intestines of a cow, paunch

*Renge:*, hungry, in want of, be desirous for, poor

*Renge: lái:*, hungry

*Renge: rábáng*, hungry and cold, abject, poor

*Renge: ore:*, abject, hungry

*Renge: ákál*, famine

*Renkáu*,? to have an appetite

*Ren̲re*, a kind of fish

*Ren̲re gocho*, the whisker-like protrusions of a "*ren̲re*"

*Reráḍ*, mischief, violence

*Rese:*,? crush, tread upon

*Ret*, file, rasp, sand

*Ret„*, small bundle of medicine *chun*, &c., a packet

*Reṭhá reṭhí*, enmity, ill-feeling, squabble, disagreement

*Reṭhe*, small, dwarfish

*Reṭhe tárup*, small kind of tiger

*Ret rette*, in line

*Ret ret ále, enále, ket koái*, put into line

*Riáu: ále, riáu enále, kedále*, consult, make up a story, come to a determination

*Riáu rájoṭ*, council, determination, plan, opinions

*Ribi: ribi: edái, kedái*, sprinkle, ooze out, drop

*Ribŏng kŏbŏng*, decrepit, aged, weak through sickness

*Richí*,* a bird of prey

*Rído: á, rít„ ená, kedái*, grind, pulverize [powder

*Rít„ lemeng*, grind to

*Riḍedo:ái, riḍet,, enái, kedeái,* be pinched, be caught, be hindered, be crushed by a weight, be squeezed, be jammed

*Rigám chágám,* noise of some one coming slowly along

*Rigdáu: á, rigdáu ená, kedeái,* drag, push, scrape along

*Righí: á, righí enái, kedái,* make a ring (in wood)

*Righí,* a ring made on wood either for ornament or as a stop

*Rijháu:ái, rijháu enái, kedeái,* sway, influence, have a bias, please

*Rijo:ái, rij enái, kedeái,*° desire

*Rilá málá,* clear, open, pure, spotless, innocent

*Rimí kedeái,* find a dead animal in the jungle (as a cow torn by tiger, &c.)

*Rimí tingi:ái, tingi enái,* exult, be merry, dance for joy

*Rímílo: á, rímíl kedái,* cloud

*Rímíl,* cloud

*Rímíl sáḍe,* thunder

*Rín,*° credit

*Rín jom,* borrow

*Rín ṭaká,* debt

*Rín topá:,* forgive debts

*Ringáu:ái, ringáu enái, kedeái,* soar, sing with high voice

*Ripit,,* eyelid

*Ripipijo: áling, ripipi: enáling,* wink, make signs with eyes mutually

*Riṛh,* ridge (of field), edge of something bevilled

*Risá sím,* hen with feathers standing forward

*Rochodo:ái, rochot,, enái, kedeái,* break (as head on a tree)

*Rodo: ái, rot,, enái, kedeái,* tie hair in a knot, arrange hair or whiskers

*Roḍojo: á, roḍoi: ená, kedái,* drop (as rain, &c.), wring out

*Roḍgo,* stony ground; a kind of fish

*Rofhái eái, enái, kedeái,*° be reconciled, be established in a place

*Rog,, ái, ro: ená, kedái,* punch, make holes, prick, sew, pierce, gore, goad, cut with chisel

*Ro: mid,,,* sew on, repair

*Ro: eset,,* sew up

*Ro:bhugag,* pierce a hole

*Rogá,* disease, ulcers

*Rog bighin,* sickness

*Rogi*, sick, diseased

*Rogoṛ*, a stream

*Rŏgŏṛte*, steadily, uniformly, continually

*Rohed eái, rohet,, kedái*, quarrel, reproach, upbraid, reprove, abuse, scold (see also *ruhed*)

*Rohoi: á, rohoi kedái*, plant

*Rohon*, occupation (see *rahan*)

*Rohoṛo: á, rohoṛ ená, kedeái*, dry, wither

*Rohoṛ khaṛangáu: á, khaṛangáu ená*, dry up

*Rohoṛ*, dry, crisp, dried up

*Roká*, freshly made

*Rohoi:*, a small snail

*Rŏkŏm*,[o] sort

*Rokoṛo:ái, rokoṛ kedeái*, sleep on something rough so as to pain the body

*Rol*, an astringent fruit used in tanning "kasáphal"

*Rol muiṇ*, black ant

*Rolo: á, rol ená, kedeái*, take meat off the fire, fall or come out of fire

*Romjhom*,? anklet

*Rongo: á, rongoi ená, rongo kedeái*, burn up, singe, scorch, wither, singe the bristles of a pig, or feathers of a chicken

*Rŏpdhŏp ái, hedeái*, conceal a fault, connive

*Ropo: ákin, ropo enákin*, fight (as bulls) mutually stick, argue (see *rog,,*)

*Ropoṛ áling, enáling*, converse, fight (in words), argue, quarrel (see *roṛ*)

*Ropoṛá:* conversation, quarrel, argument

*Roṛ*, speech

*Roṛ ái, ádeái, kedeái*, speak, explain, relate, mention, talk

*Roṛ jong*, converse

*Roṛ sahí*, testify

*Roṛ ruaṛ*, answer

*Roṛ sáḍe*, preach, proclaim

*Roṛ párom*, provoke by speaking rudely

*Roṛ sohod,,*, advocate, plead another's cause

*Roṛ lánd*, life, walk, conversation, consummation of marriage

*Roṛ suk*, abuse, provoke

*Roṛ midá:*, determination, arranged plan

*Ros*,[o] juice

*Rŏse rŏsete*, gently, softly, slowly

*Rŏsŏm rŏsŏm*, indisposed, slightly unwell, gently, quietly,

*Roṭe*, frog, toad; to singe? heat?

*Rúạ*, disease, fever, sick, ill

*Rúạ háso*, sickness, pain

*Rúaṛ*, back, again (adverb)

*Ruaṛo:ái, ruaṛ enái, hedeái*, return, turn, bring back, change

*Rúbo: á, rúp,, ená, kedeái*, blow down, uproot by storm, knock down, push over

*Rúchup,, rúchup,,*, crackling in eating something hard

*Ruhed eái, ruhet,, kedeái*, abuse, scold, quarrel, reproach, reprove, upbraid

*Ru: hedi:*, reviler, calumniator, accuser

*Ruhi*, "rui" a kind of fish

*Rúi*† cotton (of the country)

*Rúkạ*,° chisel

*Rukhiạ:ái, rukhiạ ená, kedeái*, be saved, be preserved, escape

*Ruk rábon*, scarcity, destitution

*Ruku: á, rukui ená, ruku kedeái*, shake, swing

*Rumbui: chumbujo: ále, chumbui: enále*, be festive, keep festival

*Rumu:ái, rum enái, kedeái*, shake the head (the custom in worshipping)

*Rund runáu:ái, runáu enái, kedeái*, shiver with cold

*Rundá*,* a wild cat

*Rúpạ*,† silver

S

*Sabágo: á, sabá: ená, kedái*, be tasteless, become insipid

*Saḅásí*, greatness, glory, praise, renown

*Sabási ái, enái, ocho kedeái*, praise

*Sábít*,† excellent

*Sábo: ái, sáp,, enái, kedeái*, catch, arrest, discover

*Sásápí:*, catcher

*Sábudo: á, sábut,, ená, kedeái*,° give evidence, prove, settle

*Sádá*,† plain (adj.), pure, unmixed

*Sáḍe*, sound, voice, marriage portion

*Sáḍe:ái, sáḍe enái, kedái*, give a sound

*Sáḍ*, utter, speak loudly

*Sadháu:ái, sadháu enái, het táiá*, commit suicide

*Sádom*, horse

*Sádom muíṇ*, red ant

*Sáe kedái*, finish

*Sáegát,,*, rough, uneven, not smooth

*Saṅgát,, roṛ*, speak irritatingly, vex

*Safhạí ái, safhá ená kedeái*,[o] clean, cleanse, purify, sanctify, give explanation

*Ságá:*, a kind of early grass

*Ságáṛ*, cart

*Ságeno: á, ságen ená, kedái*, bud, grow

*Sagui: bagui:*, disorderly conduct, confusion, uncertainty

*Ságuno: á, ságun ená, ádeái*, arrange marriages, be successful, lucky, arrange anything

*Sáhạí ái, ái, ádeái*, bless, praise, thank, help, assist, favour

*Sáhán*, fuel

*Saháṛo: á, saháṛ ená, kedeái; sá: á, sá ená, kedeái*, put aside, separate

*Saháu: á, saháu ená, kedái*,[o] bear, endure

*Sáheb*,† gentleman, sir

*Sáhed ái, sáhet,, kedái*, breathe

*Sahí*, true, proper

*Sahí juhí: á, juhí ená, kedáling*, correct, arrange, fix

*Sáhobo: á, sáhop,, ená, kedái*, hold, contain, fill in

*Sahráj*,* a kind of large bird

*Sahtá*,[o] cheap

*Sái ái, ená, kedái*, remove to another place (see *sá*)

*Sạil*, wild male buffalo

*Saintáu*, to arrange

*Sáj*,† ornament, dress

*Sajai*,[o] punishment

*Sajáu:ái, sajáu enái, hedeái*,[o] prepare, train

*Sákám*, leaf

*Sakaráth*, a feast occurring about the middle of January

*Sákhí*,† witness

*Sákom*, bracelet

*Sákor*,* a kind of tree, "*sij*"

*Sakṛá*, narrow

*Sakṛí*, crumbs, morsels

*Saktí*,[o] hardship, severity

*Saktí:ái, saktí enái, hedeái*, punish, take an oath

*Sákwá*, flute of horn

*Salá ái, enái, kedeái*, pick out

*Sálágo:ái, sálá: enái, kedeái*, mix, collect

*Saláh*,† counsel, advice

*Salámí*, offering, present to a great man

*Sálás*, rare, new, strange, novel

*Sálás kathá*, a discovery

*Salá saláte*, with

*Salgáu: á, salgáu ená, kedái*[o], set fire, kindle, lighten

*Sámá*,* a kind of wild grass

*Samá chákŏr*,* a kind of large bird

*Samágo: á, samá: ená, kedái*, cut off, cut up meat

*Sámáng*, front

*Sámángá:*, offered (in sacrifice, &c.)

*Sámángo: á, sámáng ená, kedeái*, offer up sacrifice, present before

*Sámángre*, before, in front, in presence of, in opinion of

*Sámáng se:, sámáng ren* or *reá*, opposite

*Sámáng daṭṭá*, front teeth

*Sámánom*, gold, golden, a jewel

*Sámbáu:ái, sámbáu enái, kedái*, fill up (or in), place in, hold, contain

*Sámbiro:ái, sámbir enái, kedeái*, sleep on the back, throw on to the back

*Samboṛáu: á, samboṛáu ená, kedeái*, sustain, support, contain, assist, hold up, be firm

*Sámge:ái, sámge enái, kedeái*, be accustomed to, get friendly with (after a short time)

*Samkhol*, a kind of bird, a kind of fish, "gendalia"

*Sámṭáu: á, sámṭáu ená, kedái*, roll up clothes, &c., tuck up, fold up, collect together, prepare, make ready

*Sán*, grinding-stone, or wheel; a caste of blacksmiths

*Saná edeá, kedeá*, wish, desire

*Sanám*, all

*Sanám lekáná*, every kind

*Sanám hilo:*, always, eternally

*Sanám ṭhen*, everywhere

*Sanámá:*, entireness, completeness

*Sánch*,[o] mould, frame

*Sánḍ*, bull

*Sánḍáng*, sleepy fellow (used in anger)

*Sanḍásí*,† tongs, pincers

*Sandes*, present to children, relatives, &c., offerings

*Sándi*, cock

*Sangá*, beam, rafter

*Sángárhe:ái, sángárhe enái, kedeái*, prop up, assist (a sick person), lean against, support

*Sánge: áko, sánge enáko, ket koái*, crowd, assemble

*Sánge idí*, increase (*e.g.* village, company, &c.)

*Sánge hoṛ*, a crowd

*Sanghái eái, sanghá enái, kedeái*, marry second time, marry a widow or deceased brother's wife

*Sangíng*, distance, distant

*Sáṇhái*, to investigate
*Sánk*, goose
*Sáṇrgom*, oppression
*Sántáu eái, kedeái*,[o] persecute, oppress
*Sásántáui:*, oppressor
*Sáṇw*, company
*Sáṇw hoṛ, sáṇwten*, comrade, companion
*Sáṇwte*, with, together with
*Sáṇwái ái, ená, kedái*, grow in abundance, have good crops, rain sufficiently
*Sáṇwái*, abundance, years of plenty (particularly of rain)
*Saṇwár*, level, even
*Saṇwáro:ái, enái*,[o] amend, reform
*Sáṇwráu:ái, saṇwráu enái, kedeái*, amend, reform, bring back, be reconciled
*Saṇwhá: á, saṇwhái enái, kedeái*, support (so as to prevent falling), repair
*Saṇwrá*, grey
*Sápáp*, give mutual evidence against; effects, furniture
*Sápáp ále, enále*, join hands (see *sáb*)
*Sáp, ṭhaharáu*, support (*e.g.* catch hold of a falling person or thing)
*Sápṛáu:ái sápṛáu ená, kedeái*, make (or get, or be) ready, prepare
*Sár*, arrow, reed from which arrows are made
*Saṛ*, saddle of an elephant
*Sárá*,[o] funeral pyle
*Sárám, sárámpárá*, elk
*Saráp áiái, ádeái*,[o] curse
*Sárápen*, accursed
*Sarbharáu*, move, excite
*Sárdi*, very
*Sárdi sengel*, conflagration
*Sárdi setong*, great glare
*Sáre: á:*, remaining, remainder, rest, remnant
*Sárejo: á, sáre: ená, kedeái*, reserve food for another, leave something (after eating)
*Sárháu:ái, sárháu enái, kedeái*, praise
*Sárháu leká*, praiseworthy, commendable
*Sáṛhe: á, sáṛhe ená, kedái*, bud
*Sáṛhe:*, vigorous, strong, (usually of plants)
*Sáṛhe: hoṛmo*, robust, good health
*Sarí: á, sarí ená, kedái*,† prove, ascertain, believe
*Sarí*, true
*Sarige*, truly

*Sarí ochoi*, to prove

*Sariá:*, truth

*Sariáu: á, sariáu ená, kedeái*, arrange, put in order, dress a fowl, &c.

*Sarím*, thatched roof, thatch

*Sárjom*, a kind of tree, "sál"

*Sarkár*, teacher, master

*Sárlágo:ái, sárlá: enái, kedeái*, be pierced with a thorn or splint

*Sáro: á, sár ená, kedái*, expand, blow (as flowers), open out hood (as cobra)

*Sáron*,? play tricks

*Sárreṛo: á, sárreṛ enái, kedeái*, to be full to overflowing, be brimfull

*Sárságun*,° deliberation before some great event, consultation, marriage arrangements, success, good results

*Saṛsaṛáu:*, be anxious

*Sársárjom*, a kind of "sál" tree

*Sasamṭáui:*, a reaper, collector

*Sásáng*,° turmeric "haldi"

*Sasantáui:*,° persecutor

*Sáset*,,, toil, trouble, pain

*Sásedo:ái, sáset*,, *enái, kedeái*, distress, vex, punish

*Sastá*,† cheap

*Satálá:*, for, through, on account

*Sátáu*,? open

*Sáte*, eave of a house

*Saṭo: á, saṭ enái, kedái*, be forward, fashioned, ready

*Sáṭob*, get a knock on chin so as to bite the tongue between the teeth

*Sátom*, the year after

*Sáṭ páṭ, sáṭmente*, quickly

*Satrú*,† enemy

*Sattam*, breast, dug, nipple, udder, teat

*Sáttáte*, by means of

*Sáu*,° merchant, creditor

*Sauṛí*, thatch, a grass used for thatching

*Sau sau lo*, burn brightly

*Sauthí mirich*,? pepper

*Se*, or

*Se bángá*, (yes) or no

*Se:*, side, towards

*Sejo: á, se: enái, kedeái*, incline, lean to one side, turn towards, direct towards

*Seá: á, seá ená, kedeái*, rot, decay, corrupt; metaph; conceal, keep hidden

*Sebíl*, taste, sweet taste

*Sedái*, ancient

*Sedái re*, anciently

*Sedái soro*, traditions

*Seke: seke*, tinkling

*Sekhí sekhí*, angry

*Sekre:*, a kind of berry

*Seledo: á, selet,, enái, hedeái*, to mix, unite

*Selet,,*, with

*Selimbo bahá*,* a kind of yellow flower

*Selip sámáng bahá*,* a kind of red flower

*Sendrá*, hunt, sport

*Sendrá seno:*, go to hunt

*Sendrá kárká*, a hunt

*Sengel*, fire, to set on fire

*Sengel dá:*, the Sántál idea of the great flood

*Sengel ere*, a kind of woodpecker

*Sengel mármár*, centipede ("Kángochar," yellow and black, poisonous)

*Sengel tetí*, Guinea hen

*Seno: ái, sen enái*, go, walk, obey, act upon, practice

*Seno: heju: i:*, a passer-by, traveller

*Seṇ seṇ sáhet*,? *senktoṛ*, pant, be out of breath

*Sente*,? direction of the compass

*Sepingno: á, sepingn ená, hedeái*, hold open in hand, put hand under (something to support it), hold, catch, support from beneath

*Ser*,† about two pounds

*Serále*, duck (wild)

*Seredo: á, seret,, ená, hedeái*, crush

*Serengn ái, hedái*, sing

*Seserengi:*, singer

*Sereng*, song

*Seṛeṛ seṛeṛ*, nauseous

*Sere sere: á, sere ená, hedái*, discharge matter

*Sermá*, sky, heaven, year

*Sermá ráj*, kingdom of heaven

*Sermáren ráibári*, spiritual messenger, angel

*Serom*, neck of animal, back of neck

*Sesá:*, final, conclusion, end

*Sesre*, at length, finally

*Setá*, dog

*Setá lekán hoṛ*, a vile person

*Setá:*, morning

*Setegn*, a spring

*Setengno: á, setengn ená, hedái*, ooze out

*Seṭero: á, seṭer enái, hedeái*, arrive, reach, deliver, convey

*Setong*, glare, sunshine

*Setongo: á, setong ená, hedái*, be hot

*Setop*, to nourish

*Sevok ái, ádeái*,° worship

*Será ái, kedeái,*° worship, serve

*Shŏrŏm,*° shame [fect

*Siddh,*° pay of a teacher,? per-

*Sidhi,* collect rent

*Sido: á, sít,, ená, kedái,* pick off the leaves

*Sih,* louse

*Sika,* the Sántál spots made by fire on left arm in youth

*Sikariyá,*° hunter, sportsman

*Si: kátup,* little finger

*Sikháu eái, kedeái,*° teach

*Siknat,,,*° teaching, doctrine

*Sikhláu eái, kedeái,* chasten

*Siki: siki:,* passionate (used of women)

*Siknrit,,,* mosquito [net

*Siknrit,, jhálí,* mosquito

*Síko:ái, sík enái, kedeái,* be like, resemble, copy

*Sikrí:ái, sikrí enái, kedeái,*° chain

*Sikrí,*° chain

*Sikyom bahá,** a kind of large white flower

*Silí,* hair rope

*Silping,* door

*Silping sing,* close the door

*Silung pitung,* filthy, dirty

*Sím,* cock, fowl, hen

*Sím rág,,,* to crow

*Sím hopon,* chicken

*Síma,*° border, limit

*Sing,* day

*Sing sátup,* all day, continually

*Sing mársál,* daylight

*Sing lái gnindá lái,* all day and night

*Sing,?* lion

*Sing árá,* a vegetable. "kandol ság"

*Singár payár,* evening

*Singno: á, sing ená, kedeái,* shut, shut up, confine

*Sinhásan,*† throne

*Sinit,,,* privacy, private occasion or opportunity, lonely place

*Sipahi,*° messenger

*Sípi: á, sípi ená, kedeái,* mix earth, or mortar, mix up one's rice and *dal* or vegetables in eating, pinch, take a handful

*Sír,* vein

*Sirát,, bárát,,,* very good meat

*Sírhi: á, sírhi ená, kedái,* prepare roof for thatch, spread thick boughs on the beams of a house

*Siri:,* smell (as bad fish or meat) stink

*Siri ái, kedeái,* seek for, look out for

*Siri áni:*, fortunate, lucky

*Sirjáu: á, sirjáu ená, kedeái*,[o] create, arise, be produced

*Sirom*, coarse grass used for baskets, &c.

*Siropá*, present, gift

*Sirpui: bhagwá*, very small *dhoti* (*nangoti*)

*Siṛṛi: biṛṛi:*,* a tree with very small leaves

*Siṛubo: á, siṛup„ enái, kedeái*, suck in. [The Sántál mothers fill their new-born babies' ears with water and then suck it in]

*Sísá*,† lead, metal

*Sísír dá:*, dew

*Sitet„*, beeswax

*Siṭká*, pains of childbirth

*Sitpasáre*,? disorderly

*Síy ái, si ená, kedái*, plough

*Si lahudo: á, lahut„ ená, kedái*, plough and harrow, plough and prepare land (*i.e.* take out grass, &c.)

*Siyáno: á, siyán enái, kedeái*,[o] grow up, arrive at maturity, be cunning, crafty, be well grown

*So: á, soi ená, so kedái*, pound rice, carry a plough from field to field, scent, smell

*So: rasá*, incense, perfume

*So: sunum*, sweet-smelling oil

*Sobod*, wash clothes

*Sŏbŏgo: á, sobo: enái, kedeái*, pound, pierce, thrust through, prick, beat

*Soḍo:*, a ditch, a small *nálá*, a stream

*Sodoro: á, sodor ená, kedeái*, represent, reveal, make a declaration, become public, advertise, proclaim

*Sodor re*, publicly

*Sogág ái, sogá: kedeái*, snap, peck (as birds), dart upon, strike (as snake)

*Soghor*, pretty

*Sohág*,? love

*Sohor*, red border of cloth, a city

*Sohoro: á, sohor enái, kedeái*, drag along (or down), push along (or down), make a border to a cloth, brush along before

*Soi ái, enái, kedeái*, extract, take out (*e.g.* thorns, &c.)

*Sojhe eái, enái, kedeái*, make straight, reform; straightforward, direct

*Sŏkŏjo: á, sokoi: enái, kedeái*, rinse, shake well (in hand), heave, shake from side to side (as water)

*Sokto: á, soktoi ená, sokto kedeái*,° strengthen, make firm, strong

*Solho:ái, solhoi enái, solho kedeái*,° be reconciled

*Solok*, peace, quiet, happiness

*Sŏlŏngo: á, solong ená, kedeái*, fill up, place in, be contained in

*Sombát*,,,† good news, welfare, good tidings

*Sombodo:ái, sombot,, enái, kedeái*, fall, stumble, fall on face

*Sombolo:ái, sombol enái, kedái*, prepare for journey (*i.e.* cook food, get vessels together)

*Somboṛáu:ái, somboṛáu enái, kedeái*,° bear, support, endure (see also *sámbaṛáu*)

*Sompáu:ái, sompáu enái, kedeái*,° deliver up or over, entrust

*Soná*,† gold

*Soná ágnui*, gild

*Soná chita*, leopard

*Sonḍá*, large side-teeth (of a tiger, boar, &c.), tusks, fangs (of a snake)

*Sondṛe:ái, sondṛe enái, kedeái*, push through a crowd, elbow one's way, pant

*Sŏndro*, scab of a sore

*Sone sud*, true

*Songe*, accompany, with

*Songet ená:*; companion

*Songo: á, song ená, kedái*, measure, a measure

*Sonhár*, goldsmith

*Soṇko:ái, soṇk enái, kedeái*, pant, be out of breath, tired

*Sontoro:ái, sontor enái, kedeái*, take care, be cautious, be on one's guard

*Soṇwáring*, grasshopper, cricket

*Sopo*, arm above the elbow

*Soṛhá*, a (round and hollow) plate of leaves

*Sŏṛhái ái, soṛhá ená, ádeái*, sew plate of leaves

*Sor*, near

*Soro: á, sor enái, kedeái*, be or bring near, come to

*Sorsor hoṛ, sorren hoṛ*, neighbour

*Sor dingi*, lately

*Soro á, ená, kedeái*, ordain (laws, &c.), appoint (customs, &c.), arrange, resolve, decree; determination, resolution

*Soṛom*, tasty, delicious

*Sŏrŏnjám*,° furniture &c. necessary for sacrifice, offerings

*Soros*, better, superior, more

*Soroso:á, soros enái, kedeái,* conquer, defeat, prevail, excel

*Soṛtái eái, soṛtá enái, kedeái,* sleep on side

*Soso** a kind of tree, "bhelwá"

*Sŏsrŏi,* grasshopper,? moth

*Sotá,*° fountain

*Sotog eái, soto: kedeái,* take care of a road, defend; brother next in age

*Sŏtŏyá:,* vulva fœmmeá

*Sotrá:,* have the menses

*Subho,*? a sore [abstinent

*Subud,*† temperate, moderate,

*Suḅuṭ,,suḅuṭ,,,* companies, knots of people

*Súd,*† interest of money

*Súde múle,*° principal and interest

*Súd águi,* take interest

*Suḍuro: á, suḍur ená, kedái,* spout, flow, bleed, push, fall (as water)

*Sugum sugum,* in the dark, steal along at night

*Suháṉrá ái, kedái,* adorn, be populous

*Suhiá:,*° right, corrected, established, proved

*Suhu:ái, suhui ená, suhu kedái,* appropriate to self the good deeds of others, boast falsely

*Súí,*† needle

*Sui á, sui ená,* spring up (as seeds)

*Sukái,*? °dry, squeeze out

*Sukh,*† pleasure, pleasing

*Sukhte,* happily

*Sukhá,* prophet (Sántál)

*Sukrí,* hog, pig

*Sului:,* matter in a sore

*Sulúk,* peace, friendship, concord

*Sulúko: áko, sulúk enáko,* be reconciled

*Sulúk idi,* make up a quarrel

*Suṃbaṛáu eái, kedeái,*° endure, remain firm (see *sámbaṛáu*)

*Sumjháu: á, sumjháu, kedái,* give back, give up, (land, a pledge, &c.), devote, surrender, forfeit

*Sumung,* all round, completely, entirely, finished

*Sumungo: á, sumung ená, kedeái,* finish, complete

*Sunḍ,*† trunk, snout, epiglottis

*Sunḍí gaddí,* liquor-shop, drinking house

*Sungá,* sting

*Sungá tejo,* a kind of worm that stings

*Suṉrukui:,* willow, water-plant

*Sunum*, oil

*Sunum piṭhá*, oilcake

*Sunum len*, express oil

*Sunum muiṇ*, black ant

*Sunum bing*, two-headed snake

*Sunum gár*, a kind of tree

*Supṭáu: á, supṭáu ená, hedái*, turn out well, be prosperous, be plentiful

*Supoṭo: á, supoṭ ená, kedái*, cook well, impart or have a pleasant taste, support a child in walking

*Suptí*, top or end of foot, small fan to clean rice

*Súr*,° greedy

*Surogojá*,* oil-plant

*Suṛui: hor*, narrow or difficult path

*Surui: surujo:ái, surui: kedái*, snuffle, sob

*Suṛujo:*, skulk

*Súsí*, an occasion against, cause of fault, ground of complaint

*Susulúki:*, kind, peaceable, peacemaker

*Susúrbáng*, wasp

*Sutám*, thread, cotton, wire, strings of musical instrument

*Sut„ bahá:ái, bahá enái, kedeái*, weave garland of flowers

*Sut„ dá:*, hole made in sand near river in order to filter the water

## T

*Tábero:ái, táber enái, kedeái*,° do homage, fall prostrate, humbly salute, make obeisance

*Ṭáben*, pounded rice (*churá*)

*Ṭábo: á, táp„enái, kedeái*, pass through

*Táhen ái, táheṇ enái*, continue, remain, dwell

*Táheno: á*, dwelling

*Táher*, cucumber

*Táháu:ái, kedái*, fathom

*Táharáu: á, ṭáharáu ená, hedeái*, stick fast, be caught, entangled, stop, impede

*Ṭáini*, staff tipped with iron

*Ták leká*, upright, erect, motionless (applied to a man standing still)

*Tákijo: á, táki: ená, kedeái*, run against, receive a concussion (on upper part of body), stumble, be offended

*Táki:, dárám* oppose

*Ṭáká*,† rupee

*Ṭáká siropá*, present of rupees

*Tákoi ái, kedái*, spin, wind

*Tálá*, half, middle

*Tálá erá*, middle wife, (there having been one before and one after)

*Tálá gnindá*, midnight

*Tálámáláre, táláre*, amid, among, in the middle, between

*Tálá oṛág eái, oṛá: enái, kedeái*, admit into house

*Tálá ṭánḍí:ái, ṭánḍi ená, kedeái*, be astonished, perplexed, in despair, in doubt

*Ṭáláu: á, ṭáláu ená, kedeái*, spend, pass, support, live

*Tále*,° palm tree

*Tálebár*, rich

*Tálík ái, kedeái*, take care of, provide for

*Tálímo:ái, tálím enái, kedeái*,° be instructed

*Tálká*,° palm of hand, sole of foot

*Tálomo: á, tálom enái, kedeái*, overflow, flow away

*Tálsá*, skin disease (in which spots appear over the whole body and disappear in a few minutes), rubbish,? parched bread made of flour

*Tamassuk*,† bond

*Támbá*,† copper

*Támbháu:ái, támbháu enái, kedeái*, restrain, hold, be prosperous in life, be successful, get over trouble, recover from sickness

*Tambú*,† tent

*Ṭamḍáu:ái, ṭamḍáu kedái*, search for, feel for, walk about?

*Ṭamḍáu báṛái*, grope about in dark

*Támíl*,° authority, possession

*Tamtá se:*, scattered everywhere

*Tán*, kind of wolf

*Ṭán, ṭánok*, famine, scarcity, want of water

*Ṭánáu: á, ṭánáu enái, kedeái*,° draw

*Ṭánḍái ái, ṭánḍá kedái*, straddle, keep the legs wide apart

*Ṭánḍi á:*, cleared land, a plain

*Ṭánḍi: á, ṭánḍi ená, kedeái*, clear land of jungle, cleanse (a road, a room)

*Ṭánḍí jong*, go to stool

*Ṭángá*, axe

*Tángingn ái, tángí kedeái*, wait for, remain

*Tapágo:*, jerk something into the mouth

*Tápám ále, enále*, fight, battle

*Tápingyo:ái, táping enái, ket táiá,* beat the head in sorrow

*Tápís,* bold, brave, angrily, fiercely, powerfully

*Tápse:,* violent, jumping about, violently tossed up

*Tárá, tárágе,* half (see *tálá*)

*Tarak mente,* quickly

*Táṛám ái, kedái,* walk

*Táṛám,* a step

*Táṛám chikná,* footsteps, footprints

*Táṛám lánḍhu,* path made by walking

*Taṛámre,* on foot

*Táṛán ái, enái,* crouch, lie down in ambush

*Táṛáng tiṛing,* impatient, fiery, impetuous, harsh

*Ṭáṛáng ṭuṛung,* tinkling sound of pots, &c., when struck to test if they are sound

*Tárásing* / *máráng tárásing,* } about four o'clock

*huḍing tárásing,* about six o'clock

*Ṭáráu: á, ṭáráu ená, kedeái,* pile up, sweep up or together, brush along (with hand)

*Táren,* shoulder

*Táṛi,*† juice, especially of palm tree

*Tárko: á, tárkoi ená, tárko kedeái,* jolt, shake up

*Táru,*° roof of mouth

*Táru lándup,* noseless, flat-nosed

*Tárup,* leopard

*Tarwáṛí,*° sword

*Táse: á, táse ená, kedeái,* dry, be spread out, expand

*Ṭáṭ,*† sackcloth

*Tátáu:ái, tátáu enái, kedeái,* be warned, be on one's guard

*Ṭáṭáu: á, ṭáṭáu ená, kedái,* be very crisp and dry, *i.e. dhán* which breaks to pieces in cleaning it

*Ṭáṭṭí,*† a kind of screen

*Ṭaṭhámar,* sudden, momentary

*Tathá enái,* he was struck by sudden fear or surprise

*Tawágo: á, tawá: enái, kedeái,* dash down

*Táyám,* crocodile

*Táyo,* clapping of hands

*Táyoi ái, ená, kedeái,* clap hands

*Táyom máṉráng,* before,? behind

*Táyomo: á, táyom ená, kedeái,* be behind

*Táyomte,* behind, after

*Táyomse:,* backwards

*Te: á, te ená, kedái*, clean grain, winnow (the grain by letting it fall to the ground and moving the fan)

*Teáro: á, teár enái, hedeái*,[o] prepare, make or get ready

*Tegnáng*,* brother-in-law, eldest sister's husband

*Ṭehár*,? be on trial

*Teheng*, to-day

*Teheng gapá*, these times, now-a-days

*Teingno: á, teing ená, kedái*, weave cloth

*Tejo*, caterpillar

*Teke: á, teke ená, kedái*, cook

*Teke: teke:*, jingling or grinding noise

*Tekráu eái, kedeái*, earnestly ask, earnestly enquire

*Tele: á, tele ená, kedái*, gather rice under the *dhenki*

*Tele*, louse

*Tel náhán, tel khar*, a funeral feast ten days after a relative's death

*Telsaṇwár*, brown, a light-coloured man

*Ṭeme: dá:*, shallow water

*Ṭená*, cage, stand for birds

*Ṭenḍáro: á, ṭenḍár enái, kedeái*, lean, rest one thing against another, rest on

*Ṭenḍár máchi*, chair with back, arm-chair

*Tengen eái, hedeái*, bring religious offerings, worship (demons), drive a nail through the cock's head (at funerals)

*Ṭengoi:*, small axe (*kulhári*)

*Teṇgun ái, tiṇgu eái, tiṇgu enái, kedeái*, stand, be security for, go bail, settle price, fix, be firm

*Tengo thiro:*, be calm

*Tenjlo:ái, tenjlo enái, kedái*, stretch one's legs after having kept them bent for some time

*Teno: á, ten enái, kedeái*, fasten down, press down, squeeze

*Tenrejhá:*, corpulent,? fat,? swelled out as dead man

*Tepai*,* a kind of tree

*Tepedo:á, tepet„ ená, kedeái*, stop up, close up, fill up, block up, shut in

*Tepeno: á, tepen enái, kedái*, cross, put in tiers

*Teráng, ái, kedái*, shoot (with a bow)

*Terdej ái, terde: kedái*, shine (used of the moon)

*Terel*,* a kind of tree, "kendu"

*Tere tese*, abundant (as flowers thickly strewn under a tree)

*Ṭeṛhá,*† crooked

*Terom,* bee

*Terom rasá,* honey

*Ṭesá,* prop

*Tesnek,* unchangeable

*Tetáng,* thirst

*Tetángo:ái, tetáng kedeái,* thirst

*Ṭewáno: á, ṭewán ená, kedeái,* recover, find (what the person is searching for), hear news of, determine, ascertain

*Teweingno: á, teweing ená, kedeái,* suspend, hold in one's hand, hanging

*Ṭhag,*† extortioner, cheat, swindler

*Ṭhághen,* prop

*Ṭhái ṭhui,* noise (of fighting, gun, &c.), slap

*Ṭhák,* marvellous, wonderful

*Thákáu:ái, thákáu enái, kedeái,*° be weary

*Ṭhákedo: á, ṭháket„ ená, kedeái,* impede, stop, arrest the course of

*Ṭháket„ dohoi,* detain, delay

*Tháktháh,* suitable

*Ṭhák ṭhákáu:ái, ṭhákáu enái,* shiver from cold, be liberal

*Thák thákáu:,* be anxious, solicitous

*Thalí: á, thalí ená, kedeái,* stick fast, sink into mud

*Thángál thungulo:ái, thungul enái, kedeái,* waddle, be infirm (from age, sickness, &c.), be disquieted

*Ṭhángkáṭhŏṛáng,* fluently; the noise made in throwing something down (as bamboos, &c.)

*Ṭháṇw eái, enái, kedeái,*† place, establish, marry, make room for

*Thapái eái, thapá ená, kedeái,*° beat, slap, beat off dust, &c.

*Thár bhasáu:ái, thárbhasáu enái, kedeái,* do quickly, naturally, unpremeditatedly, be astonished

*Thárí,*° plate (of brass)

*Thár ke thár,* in rows, in tiers

*Thártháráu:ái, thártháráu enái, kedeái,*° tremble, shiver as in ague

*Ṭhasakáu: á, ṭhasak ená, kedeái,* remove, move, stir, put in motion

*Ṭháṭáṛ,* haggard

*Ṭhathiṉrá,* leg below the knee

*Ṭhá: ṭhog ái, ṭhá: ṭho: kedái,* strike (wood, door, &c.), strike each other

*Ṭhauká*, all sorts, all kinds (of things) collection

*Thaurá*, collection of men

*Thawágo:*, dash down (see *tawágo:*)

*Thawí*, lodge, stay, stop

*Tháyái eái, tháyá kedeái*, kick

*Ṭhebo: á, ṭhep„ ená, kedeái*, snap the fingers, fillip

*Thekáu,?* begin

*Ṭhekáu:ái, ṭheháu enái, kedeái*, employ labourers, put fuel on fire

*Ṭhekomo: á, ṭhekom ená, kedái*, stick, adhere

*Ṭhelá:ái, ṭhelá enái, hedái*, become callous

*Ṭheláu: á, ṭheláu èná, kedeái*,° push, shove, haul, wrestle

*Ṭhemá: á, ṭhemái ená, ṭhemá kedái*, gird on, put on the waist (sword-belt, &c.)

*Ṭhen, ṭhe:*, by, near (prepos.)

*Ṭhenre*, near (adv.)

*Ṭhen khon*, from

*Ṭhengá*, staff, stick

*Ṭhero:ái, ṭher enái*, be bold, forward, bad-tempered (of children), thunder out

*Ṭheṛe ṭhepe*, continually moving, wagging (as dog's tail, elephant's snout)

*Ṭheṭhámuṇ*, cross, peevish, contradictory, stubborn, obstinate, sneer, ridicule, cheat

*Thetre*, be tired?

*Ṭhík*,† just, right, correct, confirmed

*Ṭhíká ái, ádeái*,† let on contract or for hire

*Ṭhikáná*,† appointed place or distance, direction

*Ṭhikán eái, enái, kedeái*, appoint, appraise, value

*Ṭhikiṛi,?* dwarf woman, short woman

*Ṭhilí*, earthen pot or jug

*Thir hatáṛ*, adjourn

*Thiro:ái, thir enái, kedeái*, hush, wait, avoid, abstain, be quiet, silent, cease

*Tho áiái, tho kedái*, spit, expectorate

*Thoblá*, bunch (of keys, &c.)

*Ṭhok*,° a cheat (and *ṭhag*)

*Thomborot„*, corpulent, fat, squat

*Ṭhongá*, a bit of bamboo used for holding oil

*Ṭhongá sár*, a quiver, a kind of small arrow

*Thonká, thorphán*, a line or band of men

*Ṭhonoko:ái, ṭhonok enái, hedeái*, adorn self, be handsome, dress finely

*Ṭhop*, a drop

*Ṭhop ṭhop*, drop-by-drop

*Thopá* (*thope, thopi*), bunch, tassel, cluster of fruit, &c.

*Thoṛá*,† a little

*Thoṛá thoṛí*, more or less

*Thoṛá din khán*, soon

*Thŏrbŏk*,? suds, froth

*Ṭhoṛeng jáng*, shin-bone

*Thotiyá*,° slow of speech

*Thoṭrá*,° stammering, stuttering, lisping

*Thu: á, thui ená, thu hedeái*, break (as vessel, egg, &c.), smash

*Ṭhugo:ái, ṭhu: enái, hedái*, hit the head against something (also applied to pots)

*Ṭhui eái, ṭhui enái, ṭhu hedeái*, aim at, sound (as a gun), hit mark

*Ti*, hand, wrist, arm

*Ti jángá*, hands and feet, limbs

*Tiágo:ái, tiá: enái, hedeái*, shoot (with a bow), bend bow, lead by hand, reach

*Tiạro:ái, tiạr enái, hedeái*, stretch one's self, stretch out hand

*Ṭihá ṭáhe:ái, ṭáhe enái, kedeái*, walk slowly from a sore leg, &c.

*Ṭihạdo:ái, ṭihạt,, enái, kedeái*, be dependent, be supported by, derive living from (used often of a widow)

*Tíj*,° a thing

*Tíj básut*,° property

*Tík*, tick

*Ṭíkạ:ái, ṭikạ enái, kedeái*,° spot, tattoo, vaccinate; a spot, stain, the Sántál marks on the left arm

*Ṭikáu:ái, ṭikáu enái, kedeái*, stop, remain, stay

*Tikikhá*, be troubled, forsake work through bother, be bothered,• choose, have authority

*Tikin ber, tikin ṭhík*,° noon

*Tikin lo̲ṇrá, tikin erá:*, about one o'clock

*Ṭikur*, dry land, high land

*Tilá*,* a kind of tree

*Ṭilhạ*, island

*Tilming*, sesamen, oil-plant, "*tíl*"

*Tín, tinạ:*, how much, how many

*Tín hábí:*, how long, how far

*Tín re*, when, what time

*Tín tirit,,*, how large

*Tín bongá, tín chándo,* how many months

*Tín mahán̩, tin sermá,* how many days, how many years

*Tín ud̩í,* what little

*Ting eái, kedeái,* knock down (with a stone) to stone

*Tingi ái, kedái,* put wood on fire

*Tingido:ái, tingit,, enái, kedeái,* fall down senseless or suddenly, ring (as ears)

*Tingná:ái, tingná kedái,* weave (cloth)

*Tiog ái, tio: ená, kedái,* arrive, overtake

*Tipiogo: áling, tipio: enáling,* walk hand-in-hand

*Tírejuge,* eternity, for ever, eternal

*T̩irhol ái, kedái,* rub ears of corn grain in hand to get out the

*Tiriáu: áko, tiriáu enáko, ket koái,* stretch, be scattered

*Tirio,* fife, flute

*Tiris,*° thirty

*Tirishál,* indefinitely long period, ever so long

*Tirit,,,* large, great

*Tirmiráu:ái, tirmiráu enái, kedeái,* flutter, toss about in agonies of death

*Tir̩ong,* a swallow

*Tirubo:ái, tirup,, enái, kedeái,* lean on or forward, stoop, bow the head, erect (house, &c.)

*Tís,* when, whenever

*Tíshon̩,* ever, whenever

*Tíshon̩báng,* never

*Titáu,?* be exhausted, faint, become weak

*T̩it̩i hisir bahá,** a kind of red wild flower

*Titit,,,* much, many

*Titmál,?* pledge, security

*Titrí,* virgins who at a marriage rub *haldi* on the bridegroom

*Titrin̩rhí,** a kind of bird. "*t̩ent̩eá*"

*Tŏbág ái, tobá: kedái,* peck (as a bird)

*Todo:ái, tot,, enái, kedeái,* dig up, root, pick out, pull off clothes, &c., take out

*T̩od̩or,* ring on wrist

*Togoi: dat̩t̩ái ái, dat̩t̩á enái, kedái,* grin, grind the teeth, gnash

*Tohináto:ái, tohinát enái, kedeái,* make or get ready, prepare

*Tohob ái, tohop,, kedái,* take a handful (*i.e.*, as much as is grasped between forefinger and thumb in reaping)

*Tohodo:ái, tohot„ enái*, stumble, get a blow (on feet or legs)

*Tok*, cudgel, pestle

*Tok leká*, erect

*Ṭokáu:ái, ṭokáu enái, kedeái*, admonish warn

*Toke,?* eat fast, stop up mouth of vessel with hand

*Ṭoke:*, a kind of lump on the eyelid, a stye

*Ṭohlá:*, small jug

*Tolo: á, tol ená, kedeái*, bind, tie

*Tol láṭijo:*, bind the hands behind the back

*Tol urij*, bind up

*Tol idí*, carry captive

*Tol samṭáu*, fasten together, bind together

*Tol oṛá:*, prison

*Ṭolá,*† division of a village

*Ṭolá áṛerenko*, neighbours

*Tolgoiám*, wool, fur, hairy

*Tolmojo: á, tolmoi: enái, kedái*, dry up, wither, fade

*Tolmojo: á, tolmoi: enái, kedái*, dry up, wither, fade

*Ṭŏlṭŏláu: á, ṭoláu ená, kedeái*, quiver on water, dance about, rock

*Ṭonḍáng*, dried up, waterless

*Tondári*, umpire, judge, take care of

*Tondári: á, tondári ená, kedái*, to judge, settle disputes, &c., investigate (a case)

*Ṭonge: á, ṭonge ená, kedeái*, join together, knot, join the clothes of a young pair at marriage, splice, bind with iron

*Ṭonge*, joint

*Tonko:ái, tonkoi enái, tonko kedeái*, be refreshed, grow warm again, recover, pull up

*Tonol*, bond, fastening

*Topá*, to bury (the dead), wear much clothes, be abundant (as grass)

*Topá*, a grave

*Topá marán*, dead and buried, be extinguished

*Topágo: á, topá: ená, kedeái* break

*Topáṛ*, cover

*Topo:ái, topoi enái, topo kedeái*, bathe, wet, steep, dip into, soak

*Topot„*,* an insect

*Topot„, topot„ sánḍi*, cockfight

*Toprámo: á, toprám ená, kedeái*, rub with mud

*Toṛ*, squirrel, hook on end of scorpion's tail

*Toṛ eái, kedeái*, sting (as a bee)

*Ṭoráu: á, ṭoráu ená, kedeái,* finish, end

*Tormoyo,?* sit carelessly

*Toroḍáng,* fish-basket

*Toroi:,* ashes

*Torojo: á, toroi: ená, kedeái,* burn up, dry up, reduce to ashes

*Ṭoṭhá,* pergunnah, part, side

*Totká,* nape of neck

*Ṭoṭko,* bells (for cows, &c.)

*Ṭoṭo,** wild cat

*Totoro,* uncouth, uneducated, [wild

*Totṛá,* stammerer

*Towá,* milk

*Towá daká,* rice and milk, "*khír*"

*Towá nuṇnuhi:,* a suckling

*Towá dáre,* mother (tree of milk)

*Ṭoyá,* jay

*Toyo: á, toi ená, kedái,* to be topsided, spring up (as one end of a piece of wood, or of a cart)

*Toyu,* jackal, fox

*Ṭuạr,* orphan

*Ṭuạr amár,* orphan and friendless

*Túbedo:ái, tubet,, enái, kedeái,* fill up a hole (spoken sometimes of a guest metephorically), stop the ears

*Ṭúi,* peak of roof, top, end, summit

*Tuing goje,* kill with an arrow

*Tuingno:ái, tuing enái, kedeái,* shoot with bow, hit the mark

*Tukạ,* nest of bird, a small house

*Ṭukui:,* earthen pot, jar, jug

*Tukup,, tukubo:ái, tukup,, enái,* become old and feeble, be decrepit?

*Ṭuku ṭukui ái, ṭuku kedái,* cook in haste in a small pot

*Tulá,*[o] scales for weighing

*Tuliáu:ái, tuliáu enái, kedeái,* increase (in wealth, &c.), grow (rich, &c.), fill, rise

*Tullạm háskom,* cotton

*Túlo: á, túl ená, kedái,* take up, raise

*Tulpái ái, tulpạ ená, kedái,* cut the hair straight at the bottom, clip, sport

*Tului:,* with, in company with,

*Tului: chaláu,* accompany

*Tulujo: á, tului: ená, kedeái,* be connected with, compare

*Tumál ái, kedái,* glean

*Tumbudo:ái, tumbut,, enái, kedeái,* fall forward, tumble, stumble, fall upon, hang the head through shame

*Tumdá:*, drum

*Tumdá: rui*, beat drum

*Ṭumkí*, small round basket

*Tumul*, marrow

*Ṭunḍango:ái, ṭunḍang enái*, walk along (metaphorically used for "life")

*Ṭunḍí*, yoke (of harness)

*Ṭungáu: á, ṭungáu ená, kedái*, convey, reach to [bow

*Ṭuniáu ái, kedái*, fit arrow on

*Tunkhi ái, kedái*, take care of remember, look after

*Tunum baṛái*, grope, feel about in the dark

*Tunumo:ái, tunum enái, kedeái*, feel, handle

*Ṭuprí*,° cap, hat, crown

*Tupuingno: ále, tupuing enále*, fight with bows and arrows (see *tuingno:*)

*Tupujo:ái, tupui: ená, kedeái*, bow down, bend, lodge as grain

*Ṭupulá*, small basket

*Tuṛí*, mustard, "*sarsoṇ*"

*Tursi*,° the sacred tree of the Hindoos

*Tursi pindá*,° the tulsi shrine of the Hindoos

*Tursi jol*,° sprinkle water (originally with the tulsi tree)

*Turuk*, the Mussulmans

*Turú tuká*, litter, grass or dirt about the house

*Ṭuṭi*, arrow-head (blunt)

*Ṭuṭi eái, kedeái*, kill with an arrow, shoot with gun

*Tutiya*, mouse

*Tutkuṛiyạ*, hut

*Ṭuṭkut*,,, firebrand, piece of firewood

*Ṭuṭuri*, to veil the face, cover head

*Tuwángo:ái, tuwáng enái, kekeái*, rub to pieces,? become very tired or weak from work, wear out

## U

*Ublạ dublạ*, waste, extravagance

*Ubo: á, ub ená, kedái*, pour out, spill

*Uchạro: á, uchạr ená, kedeái*, be infectious, remove from place to place

*Uchhan*,° publish, make known, spread news

*Uchhláu: á, uchhláu ená, kedeái*,° throw up, cast, vomit

*Uchit*,† fit, proper

*Uchung*, jerk, nudge with elbow

*Udái pudái ái, kedái*, be reduced in circumstances, sink in life, be ruined, spend, waste, throw away uselessly

*Udáṇw*, report, rumour, fame

*Uḍáu:á, uḍáu enái, kedeái*,[o] fly

*Udgár*, hot, warm

*Udgár jokhái*, summer, hot season

*Udhaṛ em*,[o] to give on credit

*Udo:á, ut" ená, kedeái*, swallow

*Udugo: á, udu: kedái, ádeái*, direct, guide, show, point out, publish, make known

*Udu: káṭup*, fore-finger

*Uḍui: dubujo:ái, dubui: enái, kedeái*, splash in water as a drowning person

*Udrí*, dropsy, measles

*Uḍungre*, outside

*Uḍung agui*, bring out

*Uḍung giḍi*, throw out

*Uḍungo:ái, uḍung ená, kedeái*, put out, expel

*Udur ái, kedái*, grasp,? snore, strangle

*Uduṛ dhumá*, stout

*Uduṛ dhupuṛ*, urgently, briskly (a word used chiefly for a person dancing violently)

*Uhu*, alas!

*Uihár ái, kedeái*, ponder, remember, consider, grieve

*Ujáṛo: á, ujáṛ ená, kedeái*,[o] destroy, forsake, be devoured, ruin, desolate

*Ujo:ái, ui: enái, kedeái*, leap for joy, be moved, excited, stirred up

*Ukbukáu:ái, bukáu enái, kedeái*, be strangled, suffocated

*Ukhráu:á, ukhráu ená, kedái*, impress, imprint

*Ukhṛí, ukhuṛ*,[o] mortar to clean rice

*Ukíl*,[o] advocate, mediator

*Úl*, mango

*Ulaṭ pulaṭo: á, pulaṭ ená, kedeái*,[o] turn upside down, put in confusion, roll from side to side

*Ulṭá ulṭí: á, ulṭí ená, kedeái*,[o] turn upside down, toss about

*Ulṭáu: á, ulṭáu ená, kedeái*,[o] upset, move string of tongue as Sántál women do to their newly-born children

*Umdhí*, deep sleep, trance

*Ummadhá: á, ummadhái enái, ummadhá kedeái*, prevent, hinder, stop another speaking, stop oxen in ploughing, prevent by an order

*Umo:ái, um enái, kedeái*, bathe, wash

*Umukte*, by means of

*Umúl*, shade, shadow, spirit of the dead

*Umúlo: á, umúl enái, kedeái*, hide, conceal, shelter

*Unhabi:*, till then

*Unjokhe:*, then

*Unkhángi*, on which [time

*Unkhon*, thence, from that

*Unre*, then

*Uni*, he, that person

*Unṭ*,† camel

*Unumo: á, unum enái, kedeái*, sink, be immersed

*Úp*, hair, wool

*Úp áni:*, hairy

*Upai*,† expedient, plan, remedy

*Upál bahá*,* a kind of white lily

*Upạro:ái, upạr enái, kedeái*, stir up, excite, help

*Upạrre*,° concerning

*Upạs ái, kedái*,° fast, be hungry

*Uphlá uphlí: á, uphli ená, kedeái*, rise and fall

*Upláu: á, upláu ená, kedeái*, emerge from water

*Upi muiṇ*, ant with wings

*Úr*, slough (of a snake), skin, rind,? peel?

*Úro:ái, úr enái, kedeái*, cast the skin, be flayed, loose nail, peel, shell

*Urạlo:ái, urạl enái, kedeái*, imitate, copy, emulate, feel desire from seeing another's success

*Uṛan*, to eat (as caterpillars)

*Urgam*, warm

*Uṛi:*, a small blackbird

*Uṛiáu eái, kedeái*, punish

*Urihon*, a little animal scarcely bigger than a rat

*Urijo: á, urí: ená, kedeái*, make sure, make fast, tighten

*Urláu: á, urláu ená, kedái*, pick out, rub and take out what comes to the top (pick out the straws from *dhán*)

*Urmál*, small bells worn on wrist or ankles

*Urú*, big black flying beetle

*Urudo: á, urut„ ená, kedái*, churn, scrape, rub

*Urung bhusum*, dirty, covered with mud or dust

*Uṛut„ uṛut„*, expectant, greedy, impatient, surprised

*Usạdo:ái, usạt„ enái, kedeái*, take offence, be sullen, be grieved, annoyed

*Usạrái ái, usạrá kedái*, be brisk, actively perform, nimble, strong, active

*Usáro: á, usár ená, kedái*, widen, wide

*Usij ái, usi: kedái,* hiss (as a snake)

*Uskáu:ái, uskáu enái, kedeái,*° stir up, excite, raise, lift up, help

*Uskup,, uskubo:ái, uskup,, enái, kedeái,* turn round in bed, prepare to rise, move just before awaking

*Uskur ái, kedái,*° aggravate, exaggerate, make complaints, put wood on fire

*Usul ái, kedái,*° pay, settle a debt

*Usúl,* high, tall

*Usúlo:ái, usúl enái, kedeái,* be tall or high

*Uṭái ái, uṭa kedái,* root as a pig

*Uṭar,* some, &c. (answering to "*sá*" in Hindustáni), many

*Uṭháu: ái, uṭháu ená, kedeái,* shut up (as a shop), part, go away, leave, depart

*Uṭháu chabái,* be abolished

*Uṭhkáu idí,* take away, take off

*Uṭhulá,* top of fireplace, stones placed round the cooking-hole

*Uṭi,* joint of body

*Utingno: á, uting ená, kedái,* barter, exchange one thing for another

*Uṭkáu: á, uṭkáu ená, kedeái,* exhume, remove, dig out, root out from bottom

*Utpátáu:ái, utpátáu enái,* be mischievous,? be solicitous, eager, anxious, determined, resolved

*Utú,* seasoning (vegetables, fish, &c.)

## Y

*Yih,?* this

*Yih ái, kedeái,* do this, do so

## Z

*Zámino: ái, zámin enái, kedeái,*† become bail